What people a [barcode] Don't Drown in the Car Pool!

"In *Don't Drown in the Car Pool*, Mark Berkowitz, Psy.D., offers a resoundingly humorous and profoundly empowering strategy for parenting. Through personal examples, creative strategies and a fresh perspective, the author guides parents into an effective and collaborative position with their children. This book is a must read for any parent looking to raise great kids and have a blast doing so."

Joseph A. Michelli, Ph.D.
Author of ***Humor, Play and Laughter - Stress-Proofing Life with Your Kids***

"This handbook of joy, laughter and wisdom is a must read for every parent who longs to be more effective, more encouraged and more enlightened! (The kids will be blessed, too!)"

Glenna Salsbury, CSP, CPAE
Author of ***The Art of the Fresh Start,*** Past President - National Speakers Association.

"If you agree that parenting is likely the most difficult job you will ever be asked to excel in, then you'll appreciate *Don't Drown in the Car Pool*. This book helps us all to work at parenting smarter, not necessarily harder. Importantly, author Mark Berkowitz, Psy.D., encourages out-of-the-box thinking utilizing creativity and humor in developing quality parent-child relationships. Simply written and with great examples, this is not textbook-y and is a must for first timers or old hands."

Jeffrey I. Dolgan, Ph.D.
Chief of Psychology - The Children's Hospital, Denver, CO

"Mark Berkowitz, Psy.D. helps families to effectively communicate through building intimacy. By reading this book you will experience personal growth and enhance your joy of parenting."

"Most people claim family is their number one priority in life. Yet most parents readily admit to feeling ill-equipped to handle the awesome task of child rearing. In *Don't Drown in the Car Pool*, Dr. Mark Berkowitz offers uniquely humorous yet practical ideas to make parenting effective and, believe it or not, even fun! His creative methods and techniques will benefit kids from toddlers to teens."

"I found this book to be full of ideas that will be a gift to parents. It combines humor with highly effective, simple tools that will enhance and nurture family relationships. *Don't Drown in the Car Pool* provides expert guidance that will help reduce the stress of raising children. This book will help good parents become great ones."

"Dr. Mark Berkowitz is insightful, funny and has his own unique brand of charisma. His radio features are highly entertaining and extremely important. I recommend him highly."

Don't Drown
in the
Car Pool!

Creative ways
to raise great kids

By
Mark Berkowitz, Psy.D.
with Verna Noel Jones

Indelible Press
2250 South Yosemite Circle
Denver, CO 80231

First Edition
Library of Congress Control Number: 00-134519
1. Parenting 2. Self-Help 3. Family 4. Psychology
ISBN: 0-9674083-1-8

Cover, Illustrations and Final Interior Design: Li Hertzi
Design Consultant: Karen Saunders
Back Cover Photo: Orpheus

Manufactured in the United States of America

For Jana –
my greatest challenge
and my greatest reward.

Don't Drown in the Car Pool!

About the Authors

Mark Berkowitz, Psy.D., is a licensed clinical psychologist, father, professional speaker and radio personality who has worked with children and families for the last 20 years. He enjoys helping parents use creativity and humor to raise more responsive and responsible children. Dr. Berkowitz also works with family-friendly corporations to help them retain valued employees by helping them successfully balance work and family pressures. He has worked as a consultant to school districts, hospitals, and adolescent treatment centers and has served on several boards of directors. He is the host of the nationally syndicated radio feature, *It's A Parent To Me With Dr. "B"*. He resides in Denver, CO. with his daughter, Jana.

Verna Noel Jones is an award-winning journalist who has worked as a writer and editor for more than 20 years. As a feature writer for both *The Chicago Tribune* and *The Denver Rocky Mountain News*, she has written countless stories on children's issues, medical issues and parenting. At the *News*, she established a well-received parenting advice column written by area experts. She also was lauded for a three-month investigative feature exposing the hidden problems and hazards of day-care homes and centers. Jones also served as editor-in-chief and writer for *Colorado Homes and Lifestyles* magazine and as managing editor and writer for *Denver Magazine*. Jones lives in Aurora, CO, with her husband Jerome Grady, and their children, Tyler and Lauren.

Don't Drown in the Car Pool!

Acknowledgements

Like many authors, I wrote the book I needed to read. Verna Noel Jones, my editor and friend, encouraged me to put my ideas and experience on paper. Her talent and enthusiasm were invaluable in fine-tuning the writing of this book. I also am grateful to Christine Testolini, president of The Integrity Agency, for her support and guidance over the years, and to designer Li Hertzi, whose artistry helped to capture the spirit of this book.

Finally, I want to thank the parents. First, my own, Ruth and Joe, who always encouraged me to follow my own path. I'm indebted as well to those parents who shared their lives and families with me, providing me with insights into the unparalleled challenge of raising children.

Don't Drown in the Car Pool!

TABLE OF CONTENTS

Smart parenting is helping your kids get the most from life while they take the least out of you.

Don't Drown in the Car Pool!

Section I

Don't Drown in the Car Pool!

Creativity and Humor

CHAPTER ONE

It's Never Too Late

Healthy parent-child relationships don't just happen, they are created. Like any worthwhile endeavor, raising responsible and responsive children requires dedication, hard work and a willingness to experiment with creative approaches to parenting challenges. All parents are creative, but they often fail to recognize the power they wield through spontaneous and unique interactions with their children. However, it's never too late to enhance your creative powers and bring harmony and joy to your family life.

When you feel yourself about to explode because your child dropped your only set of car keys in the pirhana-filled fish tank, adopting a key phrase like "Hey Abbott" or just humming the "Jaws" theme may buy you enough time to avoid launching into a tirade you'll later regret. After you have delayed your

*smoldering fuse long enough to see colors other than red,
you will be in a calmer and more creative frame of
mind. This increases the likelihood that you will retain
all your fingers after successfully retrieving your keys.*

Just the thought of this might feel overwhelming to already
stressed and exhausted parents. Yet, in the long run, creative parenting
can be less draining than fighting the same battles day in and day out.

What separates human beings from the rest of the animal kingdom
is our ability to plan, strategize, appreciate humor and be creative.
Most parents underestimate their creative abilities when it comes to
shaping their children's thoughts and behavior. Often, they respond
in unimaginative and predictable ways, signaling their children to
tune out.

"Healthy parent-child relationships don't just happen, they are created."

This book helps parents to explore new horizons by adding the
elements of surprise, mystery and humor to their parenting repertoire.
The payoff is having children who actually pay attention and cooperate.

Perhaps you've experienced this scenario:

*Six-year-old Johnny is glued to his favorite television
program while Mom yells for the umpteenth time,
"Turn off the TV and come to the table!" Johnny
remains tuned into the television and has tuned his
mother out. The increasing frustration evident in her
voice keeps him glued to his seat. When she finally
storms into the room, grabs the remote control and
clicks off the boob tube, she gets Johnny's attention,
but that's about all.*

Consider this creative alternative:

After just one unsuccessful dinner call, Mom calmly walks into the den, gently turns off the television and aims the remote control at Johnny. She presses buttons as if to beam him into the kitchen. An intentionally bad imitation of Captain Kirk from Star Trek (or anything from the latest alien craze) may be all that's needed for Johnny to follow her command.

If Johnny still refuses, a reminder that television is one of those good things that come to those who don't make Mother wait just might do the trick. The road to cooperation isn't always smooth, but parents who are willing to map out such strategies are on the right track.

In the world of television, the "laugh track" is a device used to insert canned guffaws into a situation comedy to induce viewers to chuckle. Parents encounter comedic situations with their children daily, but often fail to engage their internal "laugh track" to capitalize on countless opportunities to insert humor into their lives. Instead, children's familiar annoying behaviors tend to evoke familiar irritable responses from their parents.

It doesn't have to be that way.

Laughter is the lifeblood of a parent-child bond. Virtually no relationship is completely satisfying without it. Critically timed laughter can strengthen a relationship by replacing anger with amusement.

Humor and stress share the same origin. The potential for each exists when parents don't get what they expect or desire. Whether a parent becomes upset or is amused depends on his perception of his children and events. A parent who becomes exasperated every time "it isn't happening the way I want it to" brings a great deal of stress upon himself and his family. If instead he calmly responds, "That's not exactly what I had in mind. What's my next move?" he then is taking control of the situation by maintaining control of himself. The latter approach lends itself to sometimes even being amused by situations gone awry. Because parents often can predict resistance, opportunities abound that allow you to choose how you will handle the resistance. Parents must cultivate and maintain a sense of humor when attempting to teach their children things they desperately don't want to learn. By appreciating that this choice exists, parents effectively can resolve problems by substituting humor for irritation, even if they have to dig under an overturned plate of spaghetti to find it.

For example, when your two-year-old decides to re-enact the Hansel and Gretel story by leaving a trail of sticky Gummy Bears on your expensive Persian rug, you could react by yelling as you furiously vacuum and then threaten the loss of eating privileges. Or you could clean up with something resembling a smile on your face. In the heat of the moment, the latter may be difficult. But when children at different ages do exactly what they are expected to do within their mental and physical capabilities, parents must make conscious choices about how to react, especially when the behavior is fairly harmless. If not, further aggravation and alienation could result. When this cycle of negative emotions and reactions is set in motion, parents gradually lose their ability to choose how to interact. They simply react – often with regret.

"Humor and stress share the same origin."

Parents owe it to themselves and their children to use creativity and humor to build a fun and forgiving learning environment. While it should be considered a primary parental responsibility, at best many parents consider doing so only as an afterthought. For children to make a successful transition from being disciplined to self-discipline, their parents must deliver constructive feedback and criticism in ways their children can tolerate and accept.

Parents who are competent and creative in their adult roles can be surprisingly passive when it comes to discovering the creative side of their parenting roles. Parents lose sight of the fact that they are lucky to have a child who exhibits annoying, but age-appropriate behaviors. Parents whose children do not do this have bigger worries. Laughing with your children and discovering alternative creative ways to respond to their challenges not only is more enjoyable, but is necessary for self-preservation. If you wish to laugh more with your children, you must be prepared to work at it by changing your perspective on some behaviors that easily annoy you. When parents fail to see the humor in their children's antics (or their own), often it's because they don't look for it.

It Makes Sense

We experience life primarily through five basic senses. We learn about our children the same way. "Sight" allows us the privilege of watching them grow while we look out for their safety. Our "hearing" tells us what's on their minds, which can be a mixed blessing, especially with two-year-olds and teenagers. "Touch" is the way we often communicate love and affection. "Taste" gives us a way to monitor their food, while our sense of "smell" tells us what has happened to a toddler's meal several hours after it's consumed.

Parents use other senses to teach and relate to their children. A sense of "fairness" is how we teach them the value of compromise, while "empathy" lets them know they aren't completely alone in their struggles. An equally important but vastly underutilized sense is a parent's **sense of humor.**

Think about the many times you have laughed at your child while scolding him for something he has done. Sometimes biting your lip is the only thing that keeps you from laughing hysterically. Most parents' first instinct is to suppress laughter for fear it will dilute the seriousness of their message. Parents should capitalize on their amusement and learn to integrate it appropriately with the important messages they want to convey to their children. In short, it's more important for a parent to bite his tongue than his lip.

A child can be resourceful and stubborn when pursuing something important, and he often is well aware of when and how he has gone too far. Yet he is adept at pretending he has no idea he's overstepped his boundaries. When his demands border on the absurd, a parent's laughter can help a child acknowledge that his expectations are unreasonable, even if the child continues to insist they be met. A classic example is the four-year-old who commandeers every spoon in the house before tasting her cereal. If you handle the demand in a lighthearted manner, she often will laugh with you somewhere between the eighth and eleventh utensil. And if she doesn't, what's the big deal? Eventually, you'll get them all back!

Many parents are pleasantly surprised to find that being flexible and tolerant while occasionally indulging a child's whims can result in greater flexibility and cooperation from the child. Sometimes, a well-timed laugh or a creative, zany response is what's needed to break the tension.

This requires that you "see when you look" and "listen when you hear." Otherwise, golden parental nuggets will be missed and probably lost forever. Here is a personal example to illustrate what I mean:

> *When my daughter Jana was four, she turned to me one day and said, "Daddy, I don't want to be a Mommy when I grow up." When I asked her why she responded, "Because kids are a lot of care." After I stopped laughing, I turned to her and said, "But they're worth it."*

Ever since then, when I feel myself reaching the end of my rope, I often utter in her presence, "Kids are a lot of care." Sometimes she beats me to it. Regardless, it has become a lifeboat for us and often has saved us from drowning in the anger and chaos experienced by all families.

Of course, making the transition from irritability to creativity doesn't come without a cost. You must consciously devote time and emotional energy to making this important shift. When you do, your efforts will be greatly rewarded, and your parenting journey will be much more enjoyable.

Where Do I Begin?

How does a parent develop and utilize his creative powers and sense of humor? First, you must train yourself to be aware of your body's reactions to frustration and anger. The more adept you become at identifying subtle signals such as clenched fists, muscle tightening, gritted teeth or frantically writing away for boarding school information, the more empowered and flexible you can become in managing difficult situations. You also should eavesdrop on your own thoughts. If you hear, "?8&####" or "You little . . .!!!," you should consider shifting gears.

Parents also must sharpen their powers of perception to capture those fleeting creative opportunities. While you are taking inventory of these important internal and external clues, you must remind yourself to "think funny." This helps lay the foundation for a creative intervention. Try selecting a word or phrase that strikes you as funny and can be recalled silently or aloud during stressful moments. Find your own version of "kids are a lot of care," or steal a favorite line from a movie or television show.

❋ ❋ ❋ ❋ ❋

"Making the transition from irritability to creativity doesn't come without a cost."

❋ ❋ ❋ ❋ ❋ ❋

The key to utilizing creativity and humor is to train yourself to focus on the child, not the act. This promotes intimacy and helps build strong relationships. If you search hard enough, you'll find an amused look on his face, unusual body language and words, or you'll be struck by the ingenuity of his strategy. Often, the absurdity of the situation can be enough to make you laugh if you allow yourself to surrender to that feeling. **Remember, laughing at something does not prevent you from resolving it in a serious manner.**

Laughter can help you attain a clearer and calmer frame of mind with which to evaluate your response options. When your child realizes he won't get yelled at through the following summer for something he did on New Year's Day, he is likely to be more attentive and approachable, even knowing you disapprove of his behavior. Except perhaps in a television evangelist's audiences, people are most open to listening and cooperating when words are spoken, not screamed. **If the situation or behavior requires criticism or discipline, then**

it is important to focus on the act — not the child. Despite your upset, it is often possible to be creative and use humor to create a more pleasant atmosphere after conveying a stern message. A simple smile, raised eyebrow or funny face may be all that is required to signal to a child that the "heavy part" is over and it's time to move on.

Spending Energy Wisely

Many families rely on a budget to help them manage their household finances. Wise parents can apply the same concept to help them manage their emotions. Parents should develop an "irritation budget" to help them limit the amount of energy and time they're allowed to spend becoming aggravated over relatively trivial matters. Unlike a household budget, the rewards of parenting increase as the size of your budget decreases.

Striving to parent creatively is a relative, not an absolute goal. There are moments and situations that demand firm limits and even yelling. When safety is a concern, you should respond in an alarming manner that puts fear into your child. There are, too, some days when parents simply are exhausted, less tolerant, and more likely to communicate in an angry manner. If you're having one of those days, do your best to recognize, acknowledge and manage it, then propel yourself in a more positive direction as best you can.

If you consider that creative parenting can reduce even 10 unnecessary angry exchanges to 6 or 7, then a 30% to 40% return on your energy investment should put a smile on everyone's face. You as the parent must be first to go the extra smile.

* * * * * *

"Remember, laughing at something does not prevent you from resolving it in a serious manner."

* * * * * *

If you are skeptical about your child's annoying behaviors containing humor, consider how easily neutral observers can spot it. Most people will laugh as they watch you chase your three-year-old around the supermarket while the tomatoes fly from your hands in all directions. They're likely to be skeptical when you explain that you juggle for a living. Amusement stemming from your child playing hide and seek is readily apparent to others despite your perception that your daughter is being a brat. Why such divergent, but equally justified perceptions? Because almost everything is funny when it isn't happening to you.

Awareness

It's not uncommon for stressed-out parents to walk around in a fog. We write lists to help us focus on daily responsibilities, then proceed with each activity while preserving as much energy as possible to conquer the next challenge. As a result, we often fail to appreciate life's pleasures and absurdities. This can lead us to be caught off-guard.

I speak from personal experience. During one eventful week of my life, a friend and I each walked around with the other person's credit card. Despite repeatedly being called each other's name after using the wrong cards, it didn't occur to either of us to check the credit card name. And of the 25 or so clerks who compared our signatures to the different name on the card, not one said anything to alert us to the problem. Every time I was called David, I dismissed the clerk as confused. In fact, I was the oblivious one.

To parent creatively and effectively, you must remain alert to the interactions and influences that surround you. And to successfully implement the parenting tools offered in this book, you must remain alert and aware of opportunities to experiment with them. The path to being an innovative parent begins with developing the ability to catch yourself before you respond ineffectively so you can choose a more workable intervention.

Fortunately, you have allies in this process. Family and friends often will tip you off that you need to "lighten up" or reconsider a decision. Successful parents appreciate that raising children is a dynamic and fluid process. To keep up with our challenging offspring requires vigilance. Learning to simultaneously observe your kids and yourself is no easy task. But it is a manageable and indispensable one. After having built a solid relationship with your children, you someday might even feel comfortable allowing them to use your credit card.

Objectivity

Objectivity is essential to creative parenting. This requires parents to be as realistic as possible in assessing their children's and their own tendencies and limitations. For example, a parent must know whether he has a short fuse and then manage it effectively. That parent also must appreciate the unique qualities of each child, especially if one is more sensitive to criticism than her siblings.

In reality, parents can strive only to achieve relative objectivity. It is impossible for anyone to be completely objective, and abandon all preconceived ideas. Notions such as, "I'm the parent and that makes me right," or "Boys are more difficult than girls" might preclude a parent from discovering a more effective way to be "right" or to treat sons as fairly as daughters. Building more intimate relationships requires parents to **focus on the child, not the act.** This helps parents create and carry in their mind a clear picture of each child dressed up in all his unique qualities (attractive and unattractive). When you're alone, it is important to reflect on the personality of each child to ensure that you develop a realistic and well-integrated view of his strengths and limitations.

Parents can maximize objectivity and minimize unrealistic expectations through **visualization,** a technique popular with many Olympic athletes. Simply close your eyes, take a few deep breaths to help you relax, and then picture your child. Picture him behaving in a way that usually annoys and upsets you, then picture yourself responding in a calm but effective manner.

Do you see and feel your child differently?

Do you see yourself in a more favorable light?

Does the annoying behavior seem as important as before?

❋ ❋ ❋ ❋ ❋ ❋

"Parents should develop an 'irritation budget.'"

❋ ❋ ❋ ❋ ❋ ❋

Developing objectivity and learning to increase self-control and let go of your anger will enhance your relationships with your children. When a child misbehaves, repeat this exercise to remind yourself to consider his behavior in the context of his personality, needs, motivations and spirit. After you've begun to master this, you can comfortably send him to military school for secretly ordering every cable pay-per-view event with your credit card.

Seriously, clear and realistic pictures of your children and yourself can serve as formidable anchors to prevent you from being capsized by your anger. By holding a steady course of objectivity and self-control, you are in a much stronger position to quickly change direction as you and your children explore new emotional territories. This is the essence of creative parenting. If you plot such a course, you will discover that a frequent destination will be laughter.

Acceptance

In addition to objectivity, people who use creativity and humor to help them cope share another common trait — **acceptance.** They have learned to laugh because they **accept** the reality that many things are a certain way, and there is something funny about the irreversibility of a situation. That is why the toddler running around in the supermarket doesn't suddenly stop and surprise his mother by proclaiming, "I think my behavior is totally inappropriate," before beginning a frantic search for the store manager to apologize. Accepting that your child will exhibit some unfavorable behaviors doesn't mean you must accept those behaviors when they occur.

> *Seven-year-old Brian and his father were locked in an ongoing battle about cleaning up his room. Brian's father (who I had been seeing in therapy) was working hard to find alternatives to spanking Brian, but was stumped when Brian would reply, "But I don't want to clean up my room!"*
>
> *After we discussed the notion of acceptance, he handled the situation in a creative and effective manner. Here's what he said occurred:*

Dad: *"Brian, clean up your room now!"*

Brian: *"I don't want to."*

Dad: *"Of course you don't want to. But it's one of those things you have to do."*

Brian: *"I won't."*

At this point, Dad walked over to the television within earshot of Brian and said: "I'm very sorry, Nintendo, but Brian has decided not to play with you for a while . . . What did you say? Oh, I don't know how long Brian will prefer sitting in a dirty room to playing with you. That will be his decision."

After Brian's dad made the distinction between accepting behavior versus accepting desires, he was able to tap into his creative powers to develop the technique of apologizing to the Nintendo.

Validation

Acceptance of your child leads to a related parental challenge — **validation.** This involves making a child feel okay about who he is, even when you disapprove of his behavior. Letting a child know that you accept the fact that he wants to do something doesn't give him permission to follow through with unacceptable behavior. Conveying acceptance and appreciation of feelings and desires is a precious gift each parent should give to her children. Statements like, "I understand you want to redecorate the house," doesn't mean you have to review swatches of material together. A child who feels validated by his parents is more likely to feel a sense of freedom to explore the world through his imagination. Creative interaction from parents will successfully establish appropriate boundaries for children without alienating them. Validation is a primary building block of self-esteem. Like any successful construction project, a delicate balance must be struck between the architect (child) and the general contractor (parent).

"Almost everything is funny when it isn't happening to you."

It is difficult to think about validating your children when they insist on challenging you on even the most trivial matters. In an attempt to cope, we tend to ignore the unique nuances of their personalities and respond in a generalized way. Let me illustrate this point. Imagine the pictures hanging on the walls of your home. Are they clear or fuzzy in your mind? Do you see them in detail or do you only see the overall image? It probably has been some time since you studied them closely and appreciated the images and qualities that compelled you to purchase them. If you really want to appreciate your children at different ages and stages, you should look at your children at least once a day as if you're seeing them for the very first time. This allows you to begin with a clean slate each and every day.

Have you ever considered the importance of the last thing you say to your children before they go to sleep? No matter what happened to upset you that day, the light of your love should continue to shine brightly after you turn off the lamp.

The Moment of "Ha–Ha"

Renowned psychologist Rollo May coined the phrase **"the moment of ah-ha"** to signify the time when someone unexpectedly experiences an important revelation or breakthrough. Artists and inventors who labor to overcome obstacles to their creativity often solve challenging problems when they attempt to take a break from their work. Fortunately for us, the subconscious creative mind works on holidays and even while we sleep. The unexpected laughs you enjoy with your children — moments of ha-ha — are all-important steps on your parental journey. When a parent finally appreciates the importance of humor and creativity in communication and suddenly realizes she has begun to employ them naturally, she has experienced what I call **"the moment of ha-ha."** After you've crossed this monumental threshold, it's virtually impossible to turn back. If you commit yourself to appropriately using humor during stressful moments, before you know it, those precious moments will add up to a lifetime.

One memorable situation occurred when my daughter, Jana, decided at 18 months old to lay claim to her father's belongings as "mine." One morning, she sneaked into my closet and took the concept of mix-and-match to a new level by arranging many of my shoes and clothes on the floor in a unique design concept.

When I discovered her in the middle of what appeared to be a Saks Fifth Avenue training program, I was annoyed. But after stepping back for a moment, I was struck by how cute she was and what a wonderful time she was having discovering the exciting world of fashion. I could tell she was doing it for me, judging by the heartfelt way she wore a pair of my underwear on her head.

When I found her on the closet floor, proudly unveiling her summer collection, I quietly watched her. The Armani and Versace influences were tastefully understated. Eventually, she glanced up at me, slightly grimaced, then burst out laughing. I could tell she knew I was not elated with her choice of projects, but she also seemed to sense that her activities fell within the realm of borderline acceptable behavior.

I said her name in a serious tone, but soon laughed as I sat down next to her on the floor. For the next 10 minutes, I put ties on her while she walked around in my sneakers. Her diaper seemed to tie the outfits together, helping her to complete her own unique and dramatic fashion statements. Together, we took the concept of mix and match to new heights.

I would be dishonest if I claimed that making the transition from annoyance to amusement was easy. I also would be lying if I said I have made the transition completely. In fact, I realized that morning in my closet that I was at a crossroads and needed to begin making some decisions about how I would respond to her future good-will gestures. Would "No" or "What do you think you're doing?" or "Don't ever mix purple with green," begin to dominate my vocabulary? Or would I be able to learn to join in her festivities – at least some of the time?

In the future, when she engaged in curiosity-driven behavior, I used a similar approach by saying her name and making a face to convey my displeasure without any angry overtones. This helped her to observe her own behavior rather than always expecting me to scold and redirect her. When I did need to stifle her actions, she was more easily redirected when I inserted humor and laughter. I also became more tolerant and accepting of a range of activities that I decided were important to her

* * * * * *
"Look at your children at least once a day as if you're seeing them for the very first time."
* * * * * *

emotional growth. Our relationship became more playful without sacrificing important lessons she needed to learn.

Summary

There is no shortage of parenting books prescribing new and ageless techniques to help parents raise their children instead of just their voices. Books professing to unlock the secrets of "How To Raise The Perfect Athletic Genius And Compliant Child" often can be found at the supermarket checkout stand. Although parenting "cookbooks" can be helpful, it is a mistake to believe that raising a well-adjusted child is simply a matter of discovering the best tips and recipes. It doesn't work for the best chefs in the world and it won't work for parents, either. The risk to parents who always believe the experts are right is to feel inadequate about their own abilities when a specific technique simply doesn't work for their child.

Parenting includes at least three miracles of creation. The first is the obvious one of creating life. The second is the process of allowing children to create themselves to the extent that genetics, environment and society will allow. And the last is the way that parents handle the challenge of actively creating a rich and enjoyable relationship with their children.

A child's existence and development will follow a unique path regardless of his parents' plans and dreams. A parent can never control "the moment of ah-ha," when his child makes an important discovery and decision about the meaning of his life. But parents do spend years preparing their children for their solo performances. Contributing creativity, laughter and understanding will help ease a child's struggle to find his or her place in the world.

What this means is that parents should tread lightly and realize that, like an orchestra conductor, they may organize, fine tune and lead the performance, but they cannot simultaneously play all the instruments. It's up to the musicians to craft their individual performances with an ear toward enhancing everybody's listening experience.

Don't Drown in the Car Pool!

The Freedom to Parent

CHAPTER TWO

Developing your Personal Parenting Style

Kids are master strategists.

They disguise their guilt in smiles that melt the heart. Children possess the genius to pretend to understand less than they really do, or to blame what is obviously their responsibility on someone or something else. This makes them more formidable opponents than parents could ever imagine. Raising them to successfully cross the bridge to adulthood represents the biggest challenge of a parent's life. Don't let their size fool you. Children are extremely clever and powerful. They can zero in on a parent's weaknesses (i.e., guilt, self-doubt) and use them masterfully to their advantage.

Kids only know to push for what they want and, until taught otherwise, believe this is their primary mission in life. Pushing is how they came into this world, and they aren't likely to abandon this successful technique unless pressured to do so, or until they discover that the costs outweigh the payoffs. The more vulnerable a child perceives his parents to be, the more likely he will try to take advantage of them. After all, kids know that if you obey all the rules, you miss all the fun.

To parents, the word "push" might stand for **P**arents **U**nder **S**teady **H**arassment. For children, its meaning probably is closer to **P**ressure **U**ntil **S**omething **H**appens. As a result, parent-child agendas often are diametrically opposed. In "healthy" families, a workable balance is achieved and children gradually learn to accept their subordinate role — until they become teenagers, of course.

While striving to be the best parents possible, moms and dads face the daunting task of trying to incorporate what they learned from their own parents — minus all of the mistakes. Essentially, raising a child is an opportunity to teach somebody else in the method you wish you were taught. In theory, it's great. Unfortunately, we do bring along the bad with the good from our childhood. Sometimes, our counterproductive learned responses and reactions to situations plague us throughout our lives. This doesn't mean that we are robots doomed to perpetuate the parent-child dramas that contributed to our inadequacies as adults. To avoid perpetuating the negative, parents must feel free to make choices, especially when they conflict with what's familiar.

Often without knowing it, we incorporate into our parenting style many of the behaviors, gestures and verbal responses to which we were exposed as children. Some, such as nodding your head "yes" or "no," or spontaneously uttering "uh-oh" when something goes wrong, are multicultural and seem to almost magically appear in all of us.

When my daughter was two, an incident occurred that highlighted this phenomenon. When her mother refused to give her a piece of candy one evening, my little angel hit her mom with an uppercut to the chin. Because neither her mother nor I were aware of any recently signed boxing contract with Don King, we quickly agreed that her behavior was unacceptable. I gallantly sprang into action by vigorously shaking my finger at her while scolding her for the sucker punch. She seemed somewhat perplexed and alternated glances between me and my finger. The look on her face was reminiscent of the reaction of an English-speaking tourist who has just received directions to the bus stop in Japanese.

I then realized I was perpetuating the ancient partnership between my index finger and tongue. As a smile invaded by face, I blurted out, "I'm not sure what this means (referring to my shaking finger), but I think I'm supposed to do it." The three of us burst out laughing and, at least for the remainder of the day, there was no more hitting.

This experience, like many others, served as an important building block in helping me to observe my own reactions and respond in a manner that is consistent with how I strive to be as a parent.

As parents, we must realize that we can choose how to respond, even while in the midst of automatically reacting to our children. Instead of choosing how to react, parents often succumb to simply reacting. To raise our awareness and make it easier to put behaviors in perspective, we must enhance our ability to be self-observant and discover humor, especially when it isn't readily apparent. As parents become more easy-going, they naturally become more intuitive, creative and flexible. This makes it easier to execute your freedom to parent and sharpen your ability to prioritize issues and intervene effectively.

*Suppose your usually pleasant three-year-old is throwing a temper tantrum at bedtime. A power struggle develops and you don't want to give in to her request for you to sit in her room until she falls asleep because you don't want to set a precedent. While this makes sense, you also have a **feeling** that your child is struggling with some unidentified conflict. Perhaps she is afraid of the dark on this particular night or simply needs affection and special attention. Despite the unsolved mystery, you decide to let her win. Although you may not be completely comfortable with your decision, you sense that giving in on this occasion may help your child. It doesn't mean that a negative pattern inevitably will result.*

Many parents who feel insecure about their parenting abilities and don't act for fear of being wrong fail to recognize an indisputable truth: **You alone are your best and most consistently available parenting tool.** Like any unused tool, it can rust, break, and ultimately cause you to lose confidence in it. However, if you learn the nuances of how the tool works, keep it sharp and use it often under diverse and even adverse conditions, you'll become more adept at the craft of parenting. You also will become more tolerant and accepting of your own mistakes as you experiment with new applications. Parents who are unnecessarily rigid and overbearing risk creating an environment where kids cooperate more out of fear than desire.

Preparing to be Annoyed

As parents expend great energy toward maintaining order, children test their ingenuity by seeking to discover new worlds. They are programmed to explore. Like adults learning to parent them, they find out much about the world through experimentation. This can be exciting for children, but often exhausting for parents. Parents are free to react angrily, but would be wise to look for amusement in their child's home-based research projects. As children and families grow and mature, many scientific principles actively influence daily life.

One ever-present concept is gravity. While very young children may be unfamiliar with the term, they are all-too-familiar with letting things go, preferably from the greatest height possible. When Sir Isaac Newton accidentally used the apple to discover gravity, he had no idea how future generations of toddlers would expand the notion to include all food groups. Food becomes more interesting to children for its aerodynamic properties than for taste. In scientific terms, flight supersedes bite. Regardless of the object a child investigates, parents have two choices: Become overwhelmed or tolerate the child's healthy curiosity.

* * * * * *

"You alone are your best and most consistently available parenting tool."

* * * * * *

Parents often ask me for creative alternatives to yelling "no" when a child engages in unacceptable behavior. The following **animal logic** worked for Cameron and his dad.

> **Dad:** *"What do you think is the funniest animal?"*
>
> **Cameron:** *"Rhinoceros."*
>
> **Dad:** *"Okay. The next time you won't stop doing something after I've asked you to stop, I'll say 'rhinoceros.' That will be your reminder to listen to me, okay?"*
>
> **Cameron:** *"Okay, Dad." (I'll humor him on this one.)*

Parents also are free to choose how to respond to annoying, repetitive questions rather than becoming increasingly irritated.

> **Mom:** *"It's time to go to bed, Tracy."*
>
> **Tracy:** *"Why?"*
>
> **Mom:** *"Because it's bedtime."*
>
> **Tracy:** *"Why?"*
>
> **Mom:** *"Because it's late."*
>
> **Tracy:** *"Why?"*
>
> **Mom:** *"Z.*
>
> **Tracy:** *"Why did you say 'Z?'"*
>
> **Mom:** *"Because Z comes after Y. Since you kept saying 'Why?' I thought you wanted to say the alphabet while you got into bed. Ready? A - B - C . . . ."*

The beauty of this technique is that it utilizes humor to

trigger a shift in thinking in a way that a four-year-old can understand. If at first she is confused, mother can explain further:

> **Mom:** *"Tracey, you kept saying 'Y' when I told you it was bedtime, so I though you wanted us to say the alphabet together. When I say it's time for bed, though, that's exactly what I mean."*

Sometimes, if you are lucky, a young child will participate in saying the alphabet with you. The child may be learning it in preschool and may know songs based on the alphabet. This technique uses creativity and another effective psychological technique — **distraction**.

> *Let's say your four-year-old son, who is fascinated by cars, always gets upset when you abruptly tell him to clean up his toys. An alternative is to literally drive him to distraction. Here's how. Keep an interesting book about cars in or near his play area. When he resists cleaning, refuse to engage in a power struggle. About ten minutes before your clean-up deadline, take out the book and begin looking through it. As you comment out loud on the pictures, engage him by asking him questions about the cars, including some you are confident he can answer. His participation will let you know that he has shifted his focus and energy, which should make it easier for you to gain his cooperation in putting the toys away. Essentially, you have orchestrated a shift from an emotional to an intellectual state. People tend to reason better and be more flexible when they aren't overly invested emotionally in maintaining a particular stance.*

On the subject of tantrums, a pre-emptive strike can prove helpful. Jack, the father of Alan, an adventurous and rather emotional seven-year-old, was experimenting with creative parenting methods to help his son control his temper. When Alan throws himself on the floor and bangs his arms and legs, Jack wondered, should he imitate him and show him how silly he looks? After some discussion, we agreed that the risk was too great for Alan to feel belittled and that the tantrum may be exacerbated. However, a modified version of this idea proved effective.

> *During a calm and enjoyable day, Alan agreed to join his dad on a secret art project. They took five sheets of paper and decorated each one after numbering them one through five. Next, Dad asked Alan to sit in a chair and told him he was going to be the judge in a special event. Then Dad threw himself on the floor and engaged in an Alan-like tantrum. While imitation may not have been the sincerest form of flattery, Alan got the message. Then they switched roles and together laughed heartily for 10 minutes.*

CAUTION: Imitation isn't always the sincerest form of flattery.

Although a playful approach worked in the above example, not all children will respond favorably. If you sense your child may be too sensitive or will feel belittled, search your creative treasure chest for a more innocuous intervention.

Often, discussing issues or even taking creative risks like Jack did can be constructive during the "cool of the moment." Kids can reflect more easily on their behavior when it is explored out of context in a fun, even silly way. This intervention helped Alan to rapidly reduce his tantrum behavior.

These are just a few techniques that can be utilized by parents exercising their freedom to parent. Although creativity is involved, the ideas are by no means the work of a creative genius. The impetus for such creations can come from parents wanting to break free of the same draining and often ineffective responses. When parents continually interact in boring and familiar ways, it can be increasingly difficult to capture their children's attention and cooperation. One inherent responsibility in the freedom to parent is to use your imagination to devise novel and effective ways to relate to your children. If you make learning a more interesting and light-hearted process, your children will become more willing students. Although it may cost you a little more time and energy, the payoff can be tremendous.

The Bill of Rights — and Wrongs!

There are no universal or objective rights and wrongs against which parents are measured. Yet parents often feel compelled to wonder, "What did I do wrong?" When your children fail to live up to reasonable expectations, it reflects directly on you and that seems unfair. Self-doubt can occur even when you believe you have done everything within your power to help them be successful. To some degree, parenthood is a game of chance. With hope and effort, you and your children simultaneously can develop a sense of you as a thoughtful, caring, and reflective parent, one who truly believes the decisions you make are in their best interest. This allows for discussion of difficult issues, helps all involved to respect the rights of others, and reaffirms that final decisions often rest with parents. This is how children learn to be flexible and accommodating in a world that will refuse to indulge them just because they cry, beg, whine or attempt to pressure others so they ultimately can win. Children are forced to gradually learn that parental decisions cannot simply be categorized as "right" or "wrong." In addition, it's important for parents to free themselves of the chains of overly critical self-evaluation. It's much more helpful to think in terms of what works and what doesn't.

When parents are upset with their children, it is easy to lapse into a "lecture mode," which allows them to remain passive and uninvolved. (If it appears they are being so attentive they're taking notes, you'd better check, because you're likely to be the subject of some unflattering doodles.) Successfully resolving parent-child conflicts has a great deal more to do with **how** and **when** you address problems than with spouting forth some famous last words such as, "I'll show you who's boss." Avoiding obvious solutions such as ultimatums based on threats and intimidation will ensure that you employ tactics that have a better chance of being "right" for your family.

❀ ❀ ❀ ❀ ❀ ❀

"It's important for parents to free themselves of the chains of overly critical self-evaluation."

❀ ❀ ❀ ❀ ❀ ❀

Creating the bill of rights and wrongs for your family should not be only about deciding what child behaviors are permissible. It also must include amendments that address how **you** can better relate to your children. If you know you often respond in ways that cause your children to shut you out, you should consider alternate methods to promote interactions that will strengthen the constitution of your family. I once reviewed a psychological report on a child with significant behavior problems. During the interview, it was reported that the mother slapped the child, who retaliated aggressively. The final written comment by the interviewer was, "I'd lose it, too, if I had a mother like that."

A well-known Gestalt notion holds that "the whole is greater than the sum of its parts." If you try to analyze how you evolved as an individual through parental influences, you cannot add up all of the yeses, nos and maybes you were subjected to and plug them into a formula that equals "you." Rather, the "you" results from the quality and nature of your interactions with your parents and whether you experienced Mom and Dad as reasonable, emotionally stable, and dedicated to making sound decisions that enhanced the quality of your life. Did they set appropriate limits and boundaries that were fair, generally appropriate, and helped equip you to deal with life as an adult? Did you experience them as approachable when you disagreed with the parameters they set? Any adult who feels his parents were sensitive to his needs without overly indulging or depriving him will be better equipped and feel freer to make decisions that will help prepare his children to handle life's pressures.

Because parents cannot control the outcome of the "whole" child, the best they can hope for is to deal wisely with the "parts" (situations, negotiations and feelings). To be successful, parents must freely experiment to learn about themselves and their children while exercising the freedom to trust their instincts. **Mistakes will be made and should be accepted and learned from — not feared.**

Creative parenting that relies on sound judgment, intuitive problem-solving and humor is the model to which parents should aspire. Understanding and appreciating the difference between **content** and **process** allows parents to create their own Bill of Rights and Wrongs.

> **Content:** *That which you're fighting about.*
>
> **Process:** *What is going on between you and your child.*

In virtually all of the examples in this book, the goal is to address the process. The messages conveyed to children are "you're fighting," "not listening," "being disrespectful," and so on. Helping children learn to recognize how their behavior affects their relationships is one of the greatest gifts parents can give. It also spares parents the burden of fighting the same drawn out, daily battles with only the object of disagreement changing.

Although parents should use whatever helpful and reasonable tools are available (books, friends, seminars, therapy and even television), they must never lose confidence in their own inventiveness. It is the talent of all great inventors to identify a problem, evaluate existing methods to address it, and ultimately devise a more effective solution.

This also is the road to great parenting. It is the responsibility of parents to invent their own parenting style. The bill of rights and wrongs holds this truth to be self-evident. A solution is "right" only until a better one comes along. But just because a new and improved solution is developed, that doesn't mean the previous answer was "wrong." Parenting is a process, and it is incumbent upon parents to utilize their freedom to parent to engage in an ongoing discovery process. Even if their discoveries don't change the world, they certainly can help their families cope with change.

* * * * * *

"Mistakes will be made and should be accepted and learned from — not feared."

* * * * * *

Rights vs Privileges

The issue of rights versus privileges must be faced immediately upon entering parenthood. Infants reserve the right to deprive their parents of sleep, which quickly earns privilege status. During early childhood, children feel free to exercise their "rights" at will. Sometimes, parents wisely give in to the moment and, other times, they stand their ground to send a message about appropriate behavior. Developing a sense of humor about your child's antics, especially when they're age-appropriate, helps parents tremendously in their struggle to establish reasonable boundaries between rights and privileges. Finding the words to communicate these boundaries is the easy part. Developing the mindset to respond to your children in creative, lighthearted ways is more difficult.

It is amazing that any child experiences difficulty in English class, given how early in life children master the concept of possessive pronouns. By twenty-one months of age, virtually all children favor the word "mine." Their comprehension of "mine" repeatedly is demonstrated by ripping objects from your grasp while exhorting this battle cry. Young children are so consumed with the concept of possession that it becomes synonymous with anything they desire, regardless of where it is or who owns it. It's not until they get older and parents ask them questions like, "Who's responsibility was it to take care of this?" that children become more discriminating and learn not to respond "mine" to every situation.

In this omnipotent stage, young children show a sense of entitlement whereby they believe their whims alone determine ownership. The guidelines for establishing boundaries between rights and privileges take shape even before children can talk. For example, a strong-willed infant of an overly accommodating parent can lead to a pattern of overindulgence that could prove problematic later in life.

Parents often lose sight of which activities and objects remain within their power to help them gain their children's cooperation. Parents become so accustomed to their children participating in various activities — building blocks, Nintendo, hang-gliding — that everybody accepts them as "rights." Parents often are reluctant to disrupt their child's routine for fear of disrupting their own. They even may feel guilty if they deny their child access to a favorite activity to convey an important message.

The key to creating a healthy balance between rights and privileges is to be able to differentiate between the two. So many parents have allowed "privileges" to become "rights" that they complain they have nothing to take away when the child misbehaves. In truth, they could help their children earn the privilege of playing a favorite activity by cooperating. But often a parent's vision is blurred because he has bought into the children's stance that "the right to bear Nintendo" is an inalienable right. When parents learn to reframe an activity as a privilege instead of a right, kids begin to make better choices. Parents also benefit by escaping the blame for "taking it away." When Junior chooses not to be nice to his sister, he chooses not to ride his bike.

Parents who fail to provide their child at an early age with a healthy framework for differentiating rights from privileges often pay a large price later for their oversight or avoidance. Children aren't spared, either. Parents who give in to their three-year-old's demand to eat a Twinkies casserole for dinner six nights a week are likely to contribute to significant gaps in his maturity level — to say nothing about the ones between his teeth. Parents who don't convey the message early that children must be both responsible and responsive will encounter greater difficulty accomplishing this later.

One way to effectively convey this message is to give a child a periodic healthy dose of reality by demonstrating that behaviors have consequences and that expressed desires aren't fulfilled automatically.

If you can address a situation with a creative twist, it's likely to have a greater impact than a familiar monologue.

A father I know shared how he was concerned that his bright son was almost failing his sophomore year in college. Here's what he said to him:

> **Dad:** *"Steven, how does $41,000 sound to you?"*
>
> **Steven:** *"That sounds great, Dad!"*
>
> **Dad:** *"Good, because that's how much money you will need to take out in student loans if you don't get your act together. I'm not paying for you to fail."*

Some situations, like the above example, are clear cut. Fortunately for parents, we sometimes feel justified in consistently conveying clear messages and expectations. Parenting is most challenging when situations aren't black and white and judgment plays a major role in a decision.

It's important for parents to reserve the right to change their minds. Because kids are constantly bombarding their parents with requests, it is common to automatically respond, "No." Many parenting books will tell you to choose your battles carefully. They also advise that after you choose them, to make sure you win them. Is this really the message and model we want to display to our children? Never compromise. Never change your mind. Always do what you want! I think not. It's important for kids to experience their parents' willingness to rethink and change their position. But all are best served when parents reverse their stance quickly instead of after a long, drawn-out battle with their kids. And when you do "give in," make sure you deposit it in your "I'm a nice parent" bank. This way, when you stick to your guns during a later argument, you can make a withdrawal and say, "Remember when I . . . Now it's your turn to do what I want."

Remaining flexible and clear in communicating boundaries to your children must be an ongoing process. If you are too rigid and unapproachable (everything is a privilege), your relationship will become more distant. And if you wait until your son is convinced he's "king" (everything is a right), you will face a formidable task in convincing him to occasionally embrace his role as one of your loyal subjects. These opposing positions are two sides of the same coin. Either can promote ongoing power struggles that can arise from even the simplest question.

Johnny: "Dad, what's the difference between right and left?"

Dad: "Son, that's a very good question. You see, right is what I always am, and left is what you'll be the moment you forget that!"

Johnny: "Keep dreaming, Dad."

ONE BILLION ONE, ONE BILLION TWO,...

Patience is a Virtue: Where Can I Get Some?

CHAPTER THREE

An Attainable Goal

We live in a highly impatient world. Asking someone to do something by yesterday often isn't soon enough. Yet people still try to be flexible and patient, at least on the surface. "Relax, take your time," is a common expression uttered by people who are thinking to themselves, "As long as you don't take mine." And these are the polite people! Add the ingredient of parenting to the mix of daily pressures and what you have is a recipe for "wit's end pie." To become more patient, it is important to pinpoint situations that lead to resentment or anger, then identify and give responses that aren't based purely on emotion.

New and expectant parents generally are aware that they will face some major stresses such as sleepless nights, illness, financial strain, and skyrocketing dry cleaning bills. But many daily occurrences with children can tax one's patience. Modern technology offers some tools of relief, such as cabinet locks, gates and outlet covers. (The relief comes only after you've run back to the store three times to finally identify the ones that correctly fit your house.) These tools help parents maintain some control while teaching children that "good things come to those who leave Mommy and Daddy's stuff alone." Current research reveals, however, that the only truly effective childproofing technique is to change the locks while your kids are visiting their grandparents. Because most parents search for alternatives to this approach, they are forced to rely on internal resources to develop patience and preserve their sanity.

Patience is essential to living in a harmonious environment. It also is the foundation for creative solutions to everyday parenting dilemmas. Patience shouldn't be confused with being an overly permissive parent. Rather it is the ability to control your emotions by strategically delaying your reactions to a situation until you can digest what's happening. Parents can express adamant disapproval without being justly accused of "flying off the handle." It is virtually impossible to approach problems in novel ways if your blood pressure is soaring and you're screaming loud enough to send your kids diving for cover. If you are expecting resistance, it is critical to prepare your body and mind to deal as matter-of-factly as possible with impending conflict. Then let the natural consequences of the behavior do the dirty work.

Mrs. K. was frustrated with her inability to get her kids to bathe without a battle. When she described herself as a "screamer," her three children concurred. One evening, the kids were surprised when, instead of screaming, she started issuing tickets to her children for being the dirtiest kids in school. Bath time gradually became a more cooperative endeavor.

Jim found himself locked in battle with six-year-old Ethan, pressuring him to admit to eating the missing cookies. One day, he picked up the telephone and, after pretending to dial, reported to the cookie police that a cookie monster was loose in his house. After he hung up, he told Ethan, "Sgt. Oreo says we shouldn't buy any more cookies until they stop disappearing before dinner." The cookie monster mysteriously disappeared.

Patience and creative problem-solving go hand in hand. As your patience increases, experimentation with creative parenting solutions becomes a less intimidating process. Success isn't measured solely by absolute cooperation. Even when an intervention fails, you still succeed at creating a home atmosphere that promotes a cooperative spirit.

As your patience and confidence increase, so should your tolerance for not always making perfect decisions. Children must learn to handle a range of parental decisions and some are better than others. Whether or not they are happy with them, they must live with them. The key to successful child-rearing is active participation and loving interaction. If these two ingredients are present, there is much room for parents to be less than perfect and still do a perfectly good job of raising their children. It is important, however, to continually work on developing patience. Without it, it will be difficult to follow your internal compass to guide you on a relatively smooth journey.

Parents think they automatically should know what to do when raising children, rather than intuitively feel what is best for a particular child and situation. Basic parenting techniques along with common sense and patient understanding should serve as the foundation to expand your parenting repertoire.

A parent who communicates in a patient, calm manner will have a much better chance to get through to his children. A professional speaker knows that unexpectedly lowering his voice sometimes achieves greater impact than increasing volume for effect. Anger and disappointment are communicated more effectively when parents remain in control of themselves. Like many things in life, there is good news and bad news about patience. The good news is that you will have numerous daily opportunities with which to practice it. That is also the bad news.

❋ ❋ ❋ ❋ ❋ ❋

"The key to successful child-rearing is active participation and loving interaction."

❋ ❋ ❋ ❋ ❋ ❋

Managing Anger

As already discussed, patience implies qualities of calmness, self-control and the ability to delay and wait. Although one may appear calm on the outside, an emotional storm might be raging inside. Learning patience isn't about learning never to feel or act angry. It is about learning to extend the time between feeling angry or frustrated and reacting so you can choose an appropriate and constructive way to respond. Remember, although it's a parent's prerogative to change her mind, it's a child's prerogative to mind the change. The reverse also is true. As parents, we continually must remind ourselves that **successful parenting hinges on our ability to engage, not enrage our children.**

Many people spend more time planning when and how many children to have than how they will raise them. That is due, in part, to not fully appreciating the magnitude of the parenting experience until it becomes a reality. As your child constantly changes, the only way to appreciate and stay abreast of those changes is to modify your responses accordingly. The challenge for parents is to continually adjust to your children while teaching them to cope with the rapid changes in their environment.

Understanding the legacy of anger in the family in which you grew up is important. Gaining insight into how directly or indirectly anger was expressed is necessary in learning to deal with anger as a parent. As uncomfortable as it feels, experiencing anger helps parents to be more effective. As parents become more comfortable experiencing anger, they can learn to manage it more effectively.

Anger alerts us to the need to be objective and think clearly to prevent emotions from clouding our decisions.

"Successful parenting hinges on our ability to engage, not enrage our children."

- Anger can provide a window into what our children are thinking and feeling when they provoke us.

- Feeling anger allows us to feel something other than powerless – and anything feels better than that.

- Anger provides us with an opportunity to remain in control when everything else feels beyond our control.

- Anger alerts us to the need for action or inaction – whatever is more appropriate.

- Anger can signal us to "lighten up" and laugh at ourselves for overreacting to relatively harmless situations or behaviors.

This doesn't mean anger is so helpful that you should establish a goal of being infuriated all the time. However, you should spend some time understanding what kinds of behaviors trigger your anger and whether your responses to aggravating behaviors are reasonable and constructive. It is difficult to criticize your children for handling anger in a manner that mirrors your behavior. Parents must be able to decide how to react, instead of always being a slave to their reactions. **Remember: While children can easily spark your anger, it is up to each parent to prevent the fires from raging out of control.**

Though some parents have trouble managing anger, others have equal difficulty acknowledging angry feelings. People cope with similar experiences differently. A household characterized by uncontrolled anger can result in one child emulating it while a sibling becomes passive and minimizes or denies angry feelings. They are two sides of the same coin, since neither is likely to help them to cope effectively.

✤ ✤ ✤ ✤ ✤ ✤
"It is difficult to criticize your children for handling anger in a manner that mirrors your behavior."
✤ ✤ ✤ ✤ ✤ ✤

Anger and patience are so intertwined that parents must learn to immediately identify when and why they feel angry. Many daily triggers can serve as a training ground for getting in touch with and managing your anger. These may be events such as receiving an audit letter from the IRS, feeling angry when your boss receives credit for a project you developed, or spending twenty minutes looking for your car keys, which you left in the refrigerator. Anger is more black and white than people realize. Either you are or you're not. It is often the degree of anger and the complexity of the relationships and circumstances that make it difficult for people to understand and acknowledge when they feel angry. If you don't understand when and why you are angry, the anger will determine your behavior before you do.

Try this anger management exercise:

- Write down three behaviors exhibited by your children that sometimes cause you to overreact.

- Write down how you overreact to each.

- Write down alternative reactions with which you can experiment for each behavior.

- Substitute the new reactions for the old reactions for five days.

- On the sixth day, sit alone in a quiet room and review the results.

- Congratulate yourself for significantly raising your parenting I.Q.

When people are uncomfortable with feeling angry, they may rationalize their feelings by saying, "It's stupid" or minimize their feelings by saying, "I'm not angry, I'm annoyed." Over the years, people have confided to me that anger is simply "too strong a word." They prefer to say, "I'm irritated." If a parent is to be successful at developing patience, she first must learn to recognize feeling angry or frustrated without camouflaging or making a value judgment about how she feels (i.e., I shouldn't feel angry about that!). It is important not to "should" on yourself.

Children can anger their parents in many ways, including being silly, uncooperative, avoidant, sneaky or sarcastic. Parents often can recognize the developing anger by taking note of their physical reactions:

- gritted teeth

- hand wringing

- creased forehead

- shuffling of the feet

- tightening muscles

- a sudden feeling of warmth (more noticeable in winter)

- increased heart rate

You might walk or chew gum faster (if you're talented enough do both simultaneously), or clear your throat emphatically (perhaps to avoid choking on your anger). The repertoire of anger indicators is extensive and varies with each person. Each parent needs to learn about his body so he can quickly identify his anger "flags" and decide how to respond. **Because parents often must respond swiftly, it is critical to develop a sixth sense about your feelings so you can constructively guide your actions as situations unfold.** Parents who have a highly developed sixth sense usually have worked at it, even if they possess natural talents that make it easier for them than for other parents. If recognizing your anger indicators is difficult, don't resent it when people who care about you view you as "anger challenged."

When you feel yourself becoming angry at your children, stop what you're doing and take three slow, deep breaths. Next, before you allow yourself to react, count to a billion. This way, your children will be grown and out of the house before you have to deal with them. If not, you're likely to forget what upset you. A more realistic approach is to begin the same way, but only count to 10 until you are confident that you are in control. It often helps to focus on a mental picture of yourself in control to remind yourself how powerful that feels. Repeat this process until you have achieved the necessary degree of calm and self-control to effectively deal with the situation. Then make your move. Periodically reviewing your personal inventory of anger indicators will help you to catch yourself before you suddenly become overwhelmed.

❁ ❁ ❁ ❁ ❁ ❁
"Don't resent it when people who care about you view you as 'anger challenged.'"
❁ ❁ ❁ ❁ ❁ ❁

The value of the counting approach is three-fold. First, the breathing allows you to continue living. Second, counting helps you to keep up with your math. Third, and perhaps most important, it lays important groundwork to think clearly when your patience is being taxed. While you are breathing and counting, you can plot a strategy similar to what a race car driver does when he hears, "Gentlepersons, start your engines."

How parents use their time immediately before they race to restore equilibrium and order is highly individual. While one parent at her wit's end might contact her travel agent to purchase a one-way ticket to the Bahamas, another might sit down, close her eyes and picture the ocean until she becomes seasick or has calmed down sufficiently to deal with her children. The latter approach may be impractical because the fast pace of life today barely allows parents time to sit down while the kids are awake.

Position-Perception Shift

Altering your physical proximity to your child during tense moments can be an invaluable way to help you maintain your patience. A concept I call the **position-perception shift** illustrates how to do this. The precise moment you observe your child engaged in unacceptable and annoying behavior, try moving to another place in the room before you respond. This forces you to delay your immediate reaction and view your child from a different perspective. Depending on the situation, move closer or further away from him. Before you begin to talk, kneel down to better engage him. Direct eye contact can increase the chances of seeing eye to eye on certain topics. Observing and approaching your children from different points in space helps broaden your overall perspective on your parenting role. It also helps to remind you that your child's anger-provoking behaviors usually aren't exhibited with malicious intent. Rather, they are attempts at self-gratification, are curiosity driven, or are a way to clarify acceptable boundaries.

When you physically put yourself at his level, it is easier to empathize and put yourself into his shoes. This doesn't necessarily alter your expectation that your four-your-old should stop playing and come to the table. But it can help you appreciate how difficult it is for young children to abruptly disengage from an enjoyable activity. If you embrace patience-enhancing tools, your stance will shift from "making" them to "helping them."

The task of developing patience is formidable, as many parents run on automatic pilot just to keep up with daily life. It is necessary to find a workable balance between reacting and strategizing so you can remain flexible and aware of your own and your child's changing needs. Using creativity and humor to change your perspective on common, annoying situations can help you to cope more effectively with irritating situations.

Going for the Gold

Throughout the book, I tout the value of talking to yourself as a vehicle for reducing tension, increasing patience and lightening up. Patience is relevant to people in all walks of life. Olympic athletes patiently train for years in the hope that success will lead to recognition and riches. Whether you are a parent or a pole vaulter, success comes only with hard work, dedication and perseverance. It helps to train yourself to look for and appreciate the humor in situations so as to relieve stress and highlight the enjoyment of parenting. When my daughter was a toddler, I was helped to develop my own light attitude by creating what I envision as "The Parenting Olympics":

The Bottle Toss: Believed to have begun in ancient Rome during the reign of Julius Caesar. The champion bottle tosser (usually under age two) is adept at giving the impression that he intends to finish drinking his bottle. He suddenly winds up, checks the location of all adults, and executes a Herculean toss in any direction. Style points are awarded for giving the impression that he doesn't know he did anything wrong.

The Hundred-Yard Crawl: This event relies on speed, agility and strategy. The child blasts out of the starting blocks and crawls at maximum speed with only an occasional glance back at his pursuer. Destination is unimportant. It is the chase that counts. When possible, dangerous obstacles should be encountered and barely avoided. This event is most exciting when the toddler athlete manages to cover half the distance to the stairwell before his parent realizes the event has begun.

The Fifty-Foot Dash: This event is run several times daily. Typically it is held when a parent sees his child (who has just begun walking) headed in one direction while the parent is involved with an activity in the opposite direction. For example, at the sound of the gun, the parent makes a mad dash to the stove to turn off the burner before the Spaghettios boil over. She then executes an acrobatic turn and runs to scoop up Junior just before he breaks great grandma's crystal vase on the coffee table. Timing, coordination and endurance are critical to a successful performance.

The Vault: This takes eighteen years to fill and just four years to empty. Hooray for higher education.

The Marathon: It begins with the birth of your child, lasts at least 26.2 years, is exhausting and you never really finish. No amount of training can adequately prepare you. Dropping out of the race is not an option.

Although these situations are presented tongue-in-cheek, numerous daily events do create stress for parents struggling to raise children in a manner that will keep everybody off the afternoon television talk show circuit. The "events" provide a good training ground for developing patience. If you manage to alter your view of even one annoying behavior through humor, you'll be surprised at how much better you'll feel. Often this requires breaking old habits. Consider the advice of diet counselors, who teach people how to change poor eating habits.

People who dunk for meatballs in their pasta are taught self-control by planning, eating slowly, putting their utensils down between bites, and chewing slowly to savor each morsel. Silent reminders help the dieter to avoid relapsing into overeating patterns. Their food is cut methodically, then slowly raised to their mouths for consumption. In essence, we retrain ourselves to perform a routine activity in slow motion.

So when your toddler hurls a pretzel stick like a javelin, you might wait to respond, size up the situation, then slowly walk over and pick it up while marking off the distance to determine if he is in contention for a medal. **Sizing up yourself and the situation before you react is key to developing patience.** After determining that no danger is involved, you should ask yourself if anything is to be gained by yelling and becoming distraught. When it comes to food and toddlers, the answer is often "no." So you may want to save your breath and exasperation, but perhaps settle for eating a few javelin sticks.

This doesn't mean that you shouldn't become irritated and change the intonation of your voice to communicate displeasure. Nor does it always mean that you and not your child must clean up the mess. It's your call as to how and when to share that responsibility. Remember that even a subtle change in your voice or a furrowed brow can communicate that a behavior is unacceptable. Sometimes it may be necessary to withhold the edible missile to make your point. But parents must preserve their energy and not overreact to situations that could be better served through creativity, humor and, sometimes, forgiveness.

Mission Accomplished

The issues of patience and anger management became real challenges for me when my daughter advanced to the Leonardo de Child stage. This is when children begin search-and-destroy missions using pencils, pens, crayons and lipstick as artistic ammunition. After commandeering the desired utensil, usually during some undercover operation, she indiscriminately destroyed any innocent surface she encountered. I had always wanted a mural in my bedroom, but I had not yet decided whether abstract impressionism was my first choice. Too late. Her behavior reminded me of a slightly modified, well-known marketing slogan, "Reach out and touch everything." I found myself on constant patrol to intercept and prevent any future acts of sabotage.

"Sizing up yourself and the situation before you react is key to developing patience."

After I completed basic training and became familiar with my daughter's methods and agents of destruction, I was ready to make my own contribution to the war effort. The writing was on the wall (so to speak), and I no longer could afford to remain neutral. This was slightly more difficult than I had anticipated. After my reconnaissance identified a drywall canvas about to be attacked, my first instinct was to sneak up, neutralize my daughter and swiftly remove the potentially destructive object from her hand. You might say we developed our own version of win, lose or draw. The problem was that she immediately wailed loudly and I was concerned she might alert other enemy forces of my presence. (I never knew if the neighborhood kids might stage a rescue operation on a moment's notice.) I also knew that even if I commandeered her weapon, a vast hidden arsenal was nearby. Because I possess little tolerance for audiological warfare such as crying, and hand-to-hand combat was accomplishing nothing, I realized that my best option was to negotiate a cease-fire. Instead of seizing her crayons, I decided to seize the moment.

> *As part of the cease-fire negotiations, I offered to trade some innocuous object such as a stuffed animal for my daughter's cache of pastels. Much to my surprise, she often was willing to barter her weapons. If she hesitated, gently helping with the exchange and removing her to another room often was successful. This tactic preserved many a wall in my house, as well as my sanity.*

Ring Around the Car Seat

One universal pastime all parents cherish is naptime. This often is the only thing that temporarily controls a child's boundless energy. Albert Einstein explained that energy is equal to mass times a constant squared, better known as $e=mc2$. Although this brilliant discovery explains many aspects of the universe, it requires modification when applied to toddlers. Parents can use the same formula, but in this case the **e** stands for excitement while **m** and **c** refer to misbehaving in the car. The **2** reminds you that it never happens only once. That's what I discovered after my three-year-old insisted on removing herself from the car seat after I had parked the car. I'm convinced a little voice in her head announced, "Let the games begin." She began running from side to side in the back seat, using the car seat as a shield to prevent me from grabbing her. Her new favorite phrase became, "I want to drive." I'm sure a video tape replay would reveal me as the frazzled parent as my daughter squealed with delight.

One helpful method in dealing with such problems is called **"mirroring."** This technique, often used by salespeople, is based on the premise that you get further with people by subtly mimicking their actions and demeanor. A perspective customer who is conservative, quiet and sticks to the business at hand will have trouble relating to a salesperson who is liberal, overly friendly, and wants to talk baseball for an hour before getting down to business. One day, during a particularly competitive game of ring around the car seat, I applied this concept by popping my eyes just above the front seat like she did, as if we were participating in the shootout at the O.K. Corral. To my surprise and delight, instead of evading me, she stared at me. Shortly thereafter, she surrendered peacefully. Other days, instead of surrendering, she plotted her escape. And some days, my only option was to drag her kicking and screaming from the car while she nursed her wounded pride. Even then, I found I was much less exasperated than if I had not experimented with a more playful approach.

* * * * *

Every parent has the freedom to parent, but with this freedom comes the responsibility to exercise it wisely, creatively, and appropriately. Learning to monitor your behavior and engage in constructive self-criticism can catapult your parenting skills to a significantly higher level. Your repertoire for something as simple as how to say "no" can be more diverse than you thought possible. Gaining insight into who you are and how you would like to change is what turns a good parent into a great one. Talking to yourself can become an art form instead of a sign that your medication needs to be adjusted. If I can borrow from an old Carnegie Hall joke, a parent asks her psychologist, "How can I enjoy my kids while they're driving me crazy?" He looks her in the eye and responds, "Patience, patience, patience."

While we all experience trying moments that remind us that parenting is no laughing matter, in fact, laughing does matter. Creative and enjoyable parenting takes the same amount of thought, planning and skill-building as any other worthwhile endeavor. Managing anger is the key to developing patience, which is critical to unlocking the secrets of your creative powers. Whether in a home or work environment, creativity and laughter depend on the degree to which both are valued and fostered by the people involved.

By now, you undoubtedly have spent time reflecting upon your parenting style. This should be an ongoing process. Parents — separately and together — must be willing to engage in some soul-searching to understand how they experience and respond to their children. Since the underlying dynamics of communication are complex and constantly evolving, it helps to break them down into some basic and easily understood factors. I have identified a handful of critical elements called **The Five Ts of Parenting.** These communication guidelines are universal. However, we will explore them in the context of parent-child relationships. The more parents become sensitive to and aware of each "T," the more successful they will become at raising responsive and responsible children.

Dr. "B's" Steps to Parenting Success

 Never stop growing as a parent.

 Practice going the extra smile.

 Don't just react - <u>INTERACT.</u>

 Focus on the child - not on the act. (Enhances intimacy)

 Focus on the act - not the child. (Enhances discipline)

 Bite your tongue - not your lip. (Don't berate, <u>relate</u>)

 Remember, parenting is not a one - way mirror.

 Be your own <u>best</u> critic.

 Practice being patient.

 Use creativity and humor to enhance your relationships with your children.

Don't Drown in the Car Pool!

Section II

Don't Drown in the Car Pool!

The Five Ts
of Parenting

An Overview

If communication is an art, communicating with children is a fine art. Parents are so busy parenting that there often is little time to explore in depth the nuances of parent-child communication. Whether parents capitalize on it or not, every day presents golden opportunities to refine their communication and parenting skills. Parents communicate with their children by what they **do** and say, and by what they **don't do** and say. As parents and children struggle to reconcile their different agendas and timetables, they communicate in subtle ways that affect how they perceive and respond to each other. Parents who are successful business communicators and managers aren't automatically guaranteed the same success at home. A company president responsible for overseeing millions of dollars will experience frustration when her two cents' worth of advice is rejected by her eight-year-old son. For this reason, it is important that parents understand and appreciate some variables that influence communication. I have focused on five, which I call **The Five Ts of Parenting**.

Before examining each variable, let's consider why such exploration is necessary. Parents struggle to negotiate compromises with their children that are reasonably acceptable to each. All parents share a common goal of trying to impart important ideas and values to their children. It is satisfying when a parent can conduct a straightforward discussion with her child and both understand and agree upon what is important. But excessive discussion also can create problems such as empowering a child too much. Talking isn't necessarily the same as discussing an issue. However, we do rely primarily on verbal communication, so creative word selection can make a difference.

> *"I'm confused as to why you don't want to play outside. I'm surprised that keeping the living room messy is more important."*

The quality of communication between adults has a long-lasting and powerful influence on children. Children of all ages key into and often model the dynamics of communication to which they are exposed. A child's style of interaction with siblings, peers, authority figures and the like often can be traced to her perception of her parents' relationships with each other, other adults and, of course, her.

Assuming we agree that the subtle aspects of communication are critical to effective parenting, it's time to delve into the variables. The Five Ts of Parenting are **Timing, Tact, Tone, Tolerance and Trust.** If even one of them is ignored in your relationships with your children, the likelihood of tension and frustration increases dramatically for all. The angrier and more frustrated parents become, the greater their inclination to use more punitive methods to gain their child's cooperation. A parent who frequently punishes tends to lose even when he wins.

Following is a brief overview of each "T," which subsequently will be explored in depth:

> ***Timing*** *is when a parent chooses to address a behavior or issue with a child. Parents often mistakenly believe that any unacceptable behavior by a child requires **immediate** disciplinary response. This isn't always true. It is important to evaluate the optimal time to address a problem to ensure the best possible outcome.*

Tact is how you elect to communicate with your children. Deciding how to approach a situation is critical to everyday parenting. Your responses to situations will vary considerably depending on your specific goal. For example, "discipline" versus "understanding" may require markedly different tactics. Even identical tactics don't guarantee identical results. Often, the results depend on the situation and temperament of each parent and child. Using a *tactic* that proved successful with one child is no guarantee that it will be successful with a different child or even the same child in the future.

Tone relates to the physical characteristics of your voice. Each person's voice is unique and usually varies with each spoken word. This variability notwithstanding, parents tend to develop characteristic ways of talking to their children. Although certain qualities of each person's voice are genetically programmed, we can dramatically alter them at will. When emotions come into play, our vocal characteristics take on a life of their own. How family members talk to each other affects their relationships and the atmosphere in the home.

Tolerance describes the limits of one's patience for situations, behaviors and feelings. Because each parent's biological makeup and family history are unique, one's tolerance level can fluctuate moment to moment, situation to situation. The same is true for children, so the family is left to struggle with how to maximize their enjoyment and avoid becoming estranged because of differences. While tolerance is innate to some extent, people can learn to manage and shape their responses to stress. Becoming aware of the *"triggers" and developing effective methods of self-control will increase a parent's ability to withstand many of the daily tribulations of parenting. Increasing your tolerance often involves "reframing" how you view a particular behavior.* **Reframing** *is a process whereby you purposely view something in an uncharacteristic way for enhanced perception and understanding. For parents, learning to identify and appreciate the humor in otherwise irritating situations is critical to reframing. Such flexibility makes it easier to parent creatively.*

Trust *is the foundation upon which your relationship with your child rests. Both parent and child must have confidence that they can confide in and rely on each other without being betrayed. Even when conflict is present, sharing a sense that each cares deeply about the other will help the relationship flourish and endure. Although people must develop trust in themselves, trust also must exist between two people for the relationship to evolve. If the first four Ts are the bricks, trust is the mortar that solidifies relationships. If trust is weak or absent, the relationship will become fragile and can be in danger of crumbling. Without trust, it will be difficult for people to remain sensitive to the other four Ts.*

Each "T" represents a choice as to how a parent will relate to his children. If you are willing to devote time and energy to contemplating and experimenting with the Five Ts of Parenting, you undoubtedly will discover hidden talents in your children and yourself. Devoting as little as five weeks to thinking about and experimenting with each "T" could benefit the entire family immeasurably. Visualization exercises can help you learn to integrate the 5 Ts. For example, during "tolerance" or "tone" week, begin each morning by visualizing yourself responding to your children in a specific situation with increased tolerance or a modified tone. Do this both with situations that end negatively and positively. Note how you feel better physically and emotionally, regardless of the outcomes. By maintaining an ongoing awareness of the five Ts, you will learn to effectively improvise helpful and even humorous responses to your children's behavior. This process is similar to the musician who diligently studies music and eventually becomes proficient enough to improvise on his instrument without consciously thinking about music theory. As always, be realistic in your expectations of your children's responses to your heightened awareness. Remember, the chances of them opening up their own charm school are slim to none.

Now let's begin our exploration of **The Five Ts of Parenting.** Try to create your own responses to the situations presented while you reflect on how you typically interact with your children. Each parent is his or her own most available and creative resource. Taking the time to understand and experiment with the Five Ts will be a giant step toward helping you tap into that invaluable resource.

Don't Drown in the Car Pool!

Timing

CHAPTER FOUR

Choosing When to Act

Everything in your family probably runs like clockwork. Most likely, though, each of you operates in a different time zone. Whoever coined the phrase "standard time" obviously didn't have children.

It often is difficult to determine the best time to discuss an issue with your child, so be prepared to be rebuffed when you approach him. When this occurs, experiment with giving him the power to choose when he would like you to approach him again.

Mom: "Johnny, we have to talk about you throwing your toys."

Johnny: "Not now, Mom!"

Mom: "I'll give you a choice. We can talk about it now, or you can stop playing until you're ready to talk. Your choice."

Often, the goal is to address the issue, not to win the battle of when the issue will be addressed. Parents do have the right to set the parameters, however, so they don't have to settle for "Check back with me during the next total lunar eclipse."

Who hasn't heard the phrase "timing is everything"? Even if it isn't everything, it certainly plays a critical role in all human experience. It can affect the outcome of a job application, a marriage proposal, attaining political office, the conception and sex of your child, or more serious matters such as finding a terrific pair of pants on sale.

When parents try to determine the best time to approach their children about an important issue, it is critical that they assess the situation and exercise sound judgment. For example, when a child is in the midst of a temper tantrum, it isn't the best time to request his help sharpening the steak knives.

When preparing to address unacceptable behavior, it helps to determine if your child is the type who responds best when "caught in the act" or during a less stressful time when a "briefing" can occur. The "caught in the act" approach begins and ends immediately following the misbehavior. "That's unacceptable" or "I'm finished talking about that" may be all that's required to redirect behavior. Other children may require a more extended "briefing" or discussion to fully process a parent's message. Often a combination can be highly effective, but make your response as brief as possible.

Children, like parents, face situations throughout the day that bring on varying degrees of stress. Although each parent must know his child's emotional makeup and patterns to determine when he is most approachable, many parents find snack time or bedtime suitable to discuss unresolved issues and parental expectations. Even if their child was "caught in the act," follow-up sometimes is required, especially if the behavior is an ongoing problem. To determine the optimal timing, you must be sensitive to how your child responds to being on the hot seat. The makeup of some children allows them to be admonished and then move on quickly.

* * * * * *
"Whoever coined the phrase 'standard time' obviously didn't have children."
* * * * * *

For some, the effects of scolding linger and cause them excessive anxiety. (Of course, creating some anxiety helps them learn important lessons.) An overly sensitive child may find it more difficult to quickly separate his emotions from the important lesson to be learned. Often, following negative criticism with a pleasurable activity such as a bedtime story or a simple hug will help everybody transition to a more pleasant atmosphere. This helps reinforce the notion that difficult issues can be discussed without lingering anger or resentment. As you will see shortly, revisiting important issues at unexpected moments is an effective way to gain your child's cooperation.

Although there are some fairly universal pre-bedtime activities such as book reading, watching television, and snack time, parents can be creative to further their agenda. The above examples are "passive" activities, where the child is primarily a "recipient" rather than an active participant. Allowing the child to play a passive role may help prepare him for sleep. But parents also can incorporate more fun and "active" evening rituals in the form of interactive imagination games.

Fly Me to the Moon

Try this game as a pre-bedtime activity.

"If you had to live on the moon, which five people and five things would you take with you and why?" Bear in mind that even if you are tired, you will have to tolerate their unique questions, such as, "Am I living in a townhouse or a mansion?" or "Do I have to mow the lawn . . .?" or "Can I leave all my teachers back on earth?" Parents and children can take turns answering. Introducing any topic of interest to the child, such as sports, food or clothes, can help involve the child in the game and lay the groundwork to discuss more sensitive subjects.

Jason: "Mom, can we play the 'Living On The Moon' game?"

Mom: "Great idea!"

Jason: "Okay. You go first."

Mom: "Jason, I was thinking that before I can focus my attention on the moon, I need to first talk to you about something that happens on earth."

Jason: *"What's that?"*

Mom: *"I'm concerned that you really don't like your brother."*

Jason: *"Why do you think that?"*

Mom: *"Well, you are always telling him he's not good at anything, that he's stupid, and that you don't want to be around him. You know he really looks up to you and you often hurt his feelings. Do you realize that?"*

Jason: *"I don't know. I don't think about it."*

Mom: *"Well, I know your brother thinks about it a lot. Sometimes when you're not around, he cries to me that you hate him."*

Jason: *"Really?"*

Mom: *"Yes. I know it's hard sometimes being a big brother. But what do you think about trying harder to be nice to him? I'll do what I can to help you."*

Jason: *"What can you do?"*

Mom: *"Well, if you'll let me, when I see you being mean, I'll just say your name. When you look at me I'll raise my eyebrows as high as I can, like this. When I say your name again, that's your reminder that you wanted to be nicer to him. Should we try it?"*

Jason*: "I'll try it. Now can we go to the moon?"*

Mom: *"Sure. And by the way, you don't have to take your brother."*

Because bedtime results in time alone for a child to think, a parent can capitalize on this by using praise before turning out the lights, "I know talking about your brother was difficult for you. I want to thank you for doing it. He's lucky to have you as a brother." Unexpected, strategically timed compliments are terrific reenforcers for kids.

Another productive time to discuss difficult issues can be when the parent and child are riding alone in a car on the way to a pleasurable activity. This conveys to the child that even when a parent is displeased with a particular behavior, rewarding activities will not necessarily be withheld as punishment unless specifically identified as a consequence. This helps avoid a threatening and punitive atmosphere and encourages more constructive discussion.

You might emphasize that you are glad to share enjoyable activities because it allows for "private time" to have fun together or discuss important issues. This helps to "normalize" it rather than turning the car seat into the hot seat. If the child's behavior jeopardizes his participation in the activity to which you are taking him, express your hope that he will work on making the necessary changes to preserve it. This remark highlights that he alone controls the outcome of the situation. Using creativity and humor can help you to capture his interest.

Dad: *(driving to a baseball game with his 10-year-old son): "Trevor, do you mind if I change your name to Ford?"*

Trevor: *"What do you mean by that, Dad?"*

Dad: *"See that car over there. It reminds me of you."*

Trevor: *"Why?"*

Dad: *"Because whoever's driving it is cutting people off like he's the only one on the road. Sometimes, that's the way you play short stop. You want to make every play, even if it means cutting off the third baseman or the center fielder. When someone else makes a mistake, you yell at him, but you really get upset when someone points out your mistakes."*

Trevor: *"Dad. I'm just trying to win every game. Besides, you tell me to go out every day and play my hardest."*

Dad: "That's true, son. But I also tell you to play fair and smart. It takes an entire team to win a championship."

Trevor: "I know, but I don't do it on purpose. I'd like to be a good team player."

Dad: "You're already off to a great start because you're thinking about what I'm saying. That's why I like our time alone on the way to the games. We can talk openly to each other without worrying about being interrupted or embarrassed. Why don't you think about our talk and see how you do during the next few games. I have a strong feeling you'll be an even better player who can really help the team."

Creativity and Time-Outs

Parents often rely on time-outs to help them maintain order in their family. While considering "timing," it is important to assess whether you tend to be too quick or too slow to respond to your children's antics. When the use of time-outs becomes the norm, parents tend to rush to employ them, often with diminishing returns.

Creative parents who respond in ways that teach their children to think ahead about the consequences of their behavior often become less reliant on time-outs. But time-outs can be valuable if their usage is understood and they are used effectively. It's a mistake to separate the "when" from the "how." Both will impact cooperation and the family atmosphere.

Let's explore this modern cease-fire technique, which has become as common in our homes as running water.

Time-outs originally were designed to allow children quiet time to compose themselves and regain self-control. However, for many parents it has become a punishment tool and takes on a negative connotation. When a child perceives it as punishment, it can inflame the situation and behavior that you're attempting to extinguish.

It is important for parents to change (reframe) their thinking more positively regarding the use of time-outs. When the topic is first introduced to your child, explain that it is a way to **help** him listen better. Explain that you understand that sometimes everyone has trouble listening and we each need time to think. Bear in mind that most parents' attempts to modify behavior are initially met with resistance. Often, a behavior will worsen in response to time-outs before it improves. Some children experience greater difficulty successfully completing time-outs. If that is the case with your child, make successful time-outs the goal and then move on to target specific behaviors.

Using a behavior chart and rewarding a child for cooperating with time-outs may be necessary. Make your goals modest and attainable. For example, begin by offering a small reward after the first successful time-out for a child who is experiencing extreme difficulty. As soon as possible, phase the reward system out and let your child's successful cooperation be reward enough.

To help a child calm himself, a parent should involve the child in discovering devices that will help him increase his self-control. Discussion of various devices (such as the "time-out spot") should occur when the child is calm, so together you can lay the foundation to resolve future difficulties.

> *One way to creatively use time out is to tape off a colored time-out square in a boring location. Next, have your child draw a funny face, "name" it, then tape the picture in the square. When your child requires a time out, simply instruct him to "go sit on Ernie's face for seven minutes." (One minute for each year of your child's age usually is sufficient.) It is important, however, that his younger brother's name isn't Ernie. After the time out, you can discuss the precipitating behavior. You also can incorporate some humor by becoming Ernie and in a funny voice exclaim, "Hey, kid, don't you have anything better to do than sit on my face?"*

The need for time-outs gradually should diminish. Eventually, you can say to your child, "Are you ready to listen to me now, or do you first need to go sit on Ernie's face?" If you are willing to parent creatively, Ernie is likely to get very lonely.

With negative behaviors, many parents may find themselves saying, "We've talked about this exact behavior several times and, despite your promises, you continue to misbehave." Parents should place the burden on the child by asking, "Have you changed your mind or do you still want to grow out of this behavior?" If the child says, "Yes," you must formulate a plan together or review the one already in place. Ask your child to make up a signal (verbal or nonverbal) for you to use to help him attain his goal.

Time-outs should be viewed as a vehicle for communication and cooperation. They are not solutions in and of themselves. How often have you observed a parent and child locked in an endless cycle of meaningless time-outs? Instead of positively shaping behavior, they serve the same purpose as the minute between each round of a boxing match – a chance to recharge your batteries and come out fighting.

By utilizing time-outs as a creative tool, you build an alliance with your child and together strive to achieve a common goal. It's important to realize that the above parent-child discussions aren't debates about whether or not a behavior is acceptable. The discussions involve how a parent and child can bring about positive change. If time-outs are a necessary interim step to building a cooperative foundation, so be it. However, continue to use our creativity and communication skills to end the need for time-outs.

* * * * * *

"Involve the child in discovering devices that will help him increase his self-control."

* * * * * *

I Was Only Trying to be Nice

Timing is critical not only when offering children constructive criticism but also when complimenting them. Consider a mother's comments to her son after watching him play baseball:

> ***Mother:*** *"I'm really proud of you, Duane. You played really hard today."*
>
> ***Duane:*** *"Mom, are you kidding? I struck out four times."*
>
> ***Mother:*** *"I know. But you swung really hard. The ball would have gone a mile if you'd hit it."*

Though the mother is trying hard to lift Duane's spirits, her choice of when to express her pride is poor. Not only did Duane dismiss his mother's praises, she gave him reason to be skeptical of future expressions of admiration. He might even think that she perceives his performance as indicative of his highest level of ability. Duane's mother didn't take into consideration his frustration and the likelihood that his self-esteem was fragile at that moment. Had she more carefully considered the timing of her praise after he played a good game, his response probably would have been dramatically different.

Consider another example:

> ***Mother:*** *"You really are a beautiful little girl."*
>
> ***Cindy:*** *(age 10): "Mom, I hate my haircut, there's this huge scab on my leg from falling off my bike and I have pink eye."*
>
> ***Mother:*** *"That's true. But to me you're still beautiful."*

It isn't the compliment of being beautiful that upsets Cindy but the timing of it. When parents express admiration, they must consider how the child probably is feeling about herself **at that moment**. Parents who fail to appreciate the importance of timing — even when positive feedback and praise are being expressed — run the risk of undermining their credibility. Their praise will ring hollow, they may be suspected of having a hidden agenda, and the level of trust in the relationship may be reduced. Parents who are "only trying to be nice" must carefully consider the timing of their good-will gestures. Although parents never can be assured that their timing will be perfect, obvious signs may exist that their timing is poor. The best way to navigate your way is to read the signs.

How Do I Know When to Help?

One issue with which parents struggle is deciding the best time to provide their children with outside help. This might involve hiring a tutor for school subjects or providing psychological help to deal with emotional difficulties. Even when parents sense the timing is right, several variables may preclude them from acting on their intuition. Obstacles such as money, moving frequently, and disagreements between spouses and children can delay assistance. Sometimes, receiving conflicting advice from others can cloud their judgment. It isn't uncommon or inappropriate in some cases for parents to wait and see how things progress before seeking assistance. Waiting to intervene often helps a child discover his own solutions to problems. But if the majority of those you respect are emphasizing the need for immediate help, be open-minded. Often, your gut feeling is consistent with the overwhelming feedback you're receiving from others. Failure to provide help or doing too little too late can be costly.

A few years ago, an 11-year-old boy named George was hospitalized under my care after engaging in numerous risky and anti-social behaviors. He vandalized his school, ran away from home on several occasions and frequently fought with peers. When George was five, his father had collapsed and died in front of him. Since then, George lived with his mother, older brother and sister, and an aunt who was a strict disciplinarian. George also was born with numerous medical problems resulting in extreme shortness of breath and orthopedic problems.

When George first entered the hospital he was angry and hostile, refused to talk to me and broke many of the rules. He had only agreed to be admitted because the judge told him "it was here or jail." The initial phase of his hospital treatment primarily involved managing his behavior. Despite his long history of anti-social behavior, George previously had never received counseling. His mother expressed regret that she hadn't sought help sooner for George, who obviously had struggled with depression and low self-esteem for many years. Only in the last two years had he begun expressing his anger through aggressive and risky behavior.

Over a period of about 10 days in the hospital, George settled down and began complying with the hospital rules. We slowly began to develop a rapport and discussed the behaviors that led to him being "locked up." He generally avoided talking about his feelings, but he acknowledged that his behavior was out of control and that he needed help to change. He also agreed to try medication, but insisted that he only wanted to return home. The treatment team instead recommended that George spend several months being treated at a residential facility in another state. The family reluctantly agreed to send him there. George was very upset, especially with me, and he made it clear he was complying under duress.

About two months after his discharge, a tiny article in the newspaper caught my eye. Its headline was, "Boy Missing." To my surprise, the article was about George, who was described as a "troubled youth with many physical problems." I learned that a month after entering the treatment center, George ran away in the middle of the night. The article appeared three weeks after his disappearance and still there had been no trace of him. About nine months later, I received a letter from George's mother. She said George had been found — shot and killed along with an older boy in California during a robbery attempt. She reiterated in the letter how she regretted not getting him help sooner and that writing to me was somehow an important part of her grieving process.

Now before you run out and hire a tutor for your nine month old or sign him up for intensive psychoanalysis, remember that George was a unique case and that help came many years too late. Unfortunately, no alarm goes off to alert parents as to the best time to provide their children with help. But there usually are small alarms that sound over the years. **Perhaps the most difficult and challenging aspect of parenting is sensing what to do when — and then acting upon it.** If you have a child who is resistant, it complicates matters even further. Should you have reason to be concerned about changes in your child's behavior or moods, talk to your child. Discreetly, solicit feedback about your child from others who know him, including siblings, relatives and teachers. This will help you establish parameters to determine the optimal time to intervene.

Your child is likely to be aware of his struggle, even if he is not yet open to help. Struggling is a critical part of a child's development. Waiting a reasonable amount of time while you assess the situation is seldom a grievous error. Remember, what you are feeling is a more accurate barometer of your child's needs than what you are thinking. Sometimes, help is needed immediately, and a child depends on his parents to realize when the time is right for them to call the shots. In George's case, he struggled for years before his mother sought help. It proved to be a fatal mistake.

❈ ❈ ❈ ❈ ❈ ❈

Parenting is like live television, where the actors must continue to perform despite any obvious mistakes. As parents, you are afforded the privilege of a front-row seat to observe where your children's talents and imagination take them (and sometimes you're unexpectedly pulled into the live action just as you're getting comfortable). This show plays continuously, moment to moment, day to day, and throughout your lifetime. Luckily, the admission is free, because you probably don't have any money left over after paying for music, dance, gymnastics and karate lessons. A child's curiosity and innocence should serve as powerful reminders to parents not to lose sight of what is most important in life — people and your relationships with them.

You're probably wondering what all of this has to do with timing. The answer is simple. To successfully fulfill the role of a parent, you must realize when it's time to reexamine your own attitudes, behaviors and relationships. Children are experts at ensuring you'll never forget how important this is. In essence, children see to it that you don't stop growing after you've grown up. Children often will tell their parents that their timing is bad. "Couldn't you have waited until I returned home? You embarrassed me in front of my friends." Sometimes, such a result is avoidable - other times not. Parents and children must learn to live with less than optimal outcomes. But parents should do their best to maximize positive outcomes by appreciating that "when" may be as important as "what" they say to their children.

In a fairy tale world, you could get your life to run smoothly simply by closing your eyes, tapping your heels together three times and repeating, "There's no place like home." The problem is, when you open your eyes on many mornings, you wish you were anywhere but home. As parents, we sometimes are impressed with our own wizardry, while at other times we wish we had a smarter brain, a stronger heart and the courage to make it through another day. Lions and tigers and migraines — oh my!

No matter what color the road you follow, be prepared for the bumps, ditches and, in rare instances, the flying monkeys that may try to whisk you away. Of course, after a particularly stressful day, you might go willingly. Parenting is a long journey with many twists and turns, and there will be moments when you fear you are lost without a clue of what to do next.

Parents usually don't become permanently lost, though they occasionally may spend a day or two feeling as if they'd been wandering deliriously across a desert. Just as the scorching sun makes you lose track of time, the torrid pace at which your children want to grow up can make it difficult for you to have confidence in the timing of many decisions. All that realistically can be expected from parents is that they carefully think through the decisions to promote the best possible outcome. Even if the timing is off, remember that children are resilient and all too soon will provide you with new opportunities to make amends.

There is a flip side to the parental timing issue. Children have their own internal maturation clocks. They will surprise you in negative and positive ways at completely unexpected moments. Because parents never have the power to reset these clocks, they must be able to tolerate the ever-changing pace. Making critical decisions at appropriate times can influence the pace, but children always will fight you for control of the throttle.

In some ways, timing is the most complex of the five Ts because each person's readiness to deal with various parenting challenges is unique. It is often difficult for two parents to work together, because even when both are committed to the same goals, their timetables often are different. The most effective parents understand and appreciate the value of their coaching role, and strive to work together as a team.

And as all great coaches know, the timing of important decisions has a tremendous impact on the outcome.

* * * * * *

As we move on to explore "tact," note how the success of many creative tactics relies on critical timing. Now that we have reviewed the importance of "when to act," let's explore how the element of surprise can work to your advantage.

Tact

CHAPTER FIVE

Turning Resistance into Cooperation

How someone approaches a situation often is critical in determining success or failure. We tend to view problems as insurmountable obstacles or, at the least, unexpected nuisances that distract us from more important and pleasurable goals and activities. Obstacles and problems plague us each day of our lives. The creative problem-solver appreciates that problems are facts of life, and can be jumping-off points for novel and creative solutions and experiences.

Each stage of a child's development contains behaviors and moments that always will be treasured and others that won't be missed. This is why, when you look through a baby book, you are likely to find a lock of hair, but almost never come across a dirty diaper. Need I say more?

Because parents never gain the complete cooperation of their children, they patiently must experiment with various interventions before deciding which ones will be most effective. Success depends, in part, on the existing rapport between parent and child and how conflict is addressed and resolved. A wide range of words and techniques will help if parents work at learning how to use them.

Experts schooled in martial arts appreciate that what appears to be a potential obstacle or threat can become an asset. In judo one relies on an attacker's force to successfully execute a flip. With children, it is important to identify and capitalize on their resistance and forceful attempts to take control of a situation. Fighting fire with fire is rarely the most comfortable or constructive solution. Both parties risk getting burned. Let's explore this notion in the context of a common parent/child conflict that involves gaining your children's cooperation in picking up their toys.

In a few scattered homes around the country, every toy can be found in its appropriate place. Most parents, however, wonder how their lovely home was transformed overnight into a minefield for minors. During the holidays, the only carpet most people see probably says "Welcome" on it and sits outside their front door (a place that, regardless of the temperature, looks more and more appealing). Unless you have chosen to decorate your home in early chaos with a tornado accent, you probably find yourself dealing with the problem of toys, toys, and more toys.

It is important to first understand what toys represent to a child. Toys mean play, and play is a fantasy world where children prefer adults didn't intrude. Through play, children not only have fun, but discover their hopes and fears and attempt to work out conflicts and disappointments. While family routines require that parents establish and preserve boundaries and expectations for the enjoyment and location of toys, it is important to realize that children do not shift gears as quickly as adults. Leaving toys exactly how a child arranged them is partly an expression of a child's fantasy life, which he alone controls. With a younger child, it also may signal that he hasn't yet integrated the concept of sharing common space. The more parents appreciate that behaviors sometimes are linked to multiple factors, the more likely they are to be **tact**ful and successful in getting their children to respond.

Putting toys away shouldn't require that a child always completely dismantles them and put them in the box, ill-fitting styrofoam and all. Abruptly ending his private journey into his imagination predictably will lead to upset and resistance. In fact, parents tactfully can ask their children **how** they would like to put their toys away. This same tact can be applied to a variety of issues such as cleaning one's room, helping with the laundry, or any other chores or responsibilities assigned to a child.

Let's return to the example of toys. A parent can inquire whether the child prefers to slowly put them away over the next fifteen minutes or quickly clean up during the last five minutes of his playtime. This gives the child the power to preserve important aspects of his private world and set his own reasonable pace while also pleasing his parents. Parents can openly express how much they enjoy seeing them play with their toys and how they like surprising them with new ones. She can state that although she doesn't enjoy telling them to put the toys away, it is a parent's job to keep track of time and ensure that other responsibilities are met. Saying, "Do you understand?" (and waiting for a response) can further the process of cooperation.

This working alliance is enhanced by the mutual understanding that both children and parents prefer play over work, but sometimes other issues take precedence. A parent can ask her children to offer suggestions as to what will help them to listen and cooperate so conflicts can be minimized or avoided. Including your child in the decision-making process can facilitate cooperation. It also reduces the likelihood of the child asserting himself in passive-aggressive ways, such as ignoring or cleaning up so slowly that the toys disintegrate before they make it to the shelves. Sometimes, children will surprise you with their flexibility, with suggestions such as, "Let me know when I have 10 minutes left." A child may request that one or both parents spend the last 10 minutes playing with him, and then assist in putting the toys away.

If constructive discussions about toys have taken place, but better cooperation is required, remind your child of previous discussions and ask him to summarize his previous commitments. This tactic of "reviewing the minutes" from previous proceedings helps children remain aware of the cooperative nature of living together. It also spares parents from easily falling into the "bad guy" role. Give the child specifics to jar his memory, if necessary, or "offer" a time out to help him prepare for the discussion.

As a parent learns to strike a delicate balance between monologue and dialogue, resistance gradually decreases. As resistance decreases, your reward will be increased cooperation.

"Including your child in the decision-making process can facilitate cooperation."

Helping Children Accept Responsibility

When a child perceives the power of his negative behavior, the balance of power can easily shift in favor of the child. Parents who regularly overreact to a child's behavior unknowingly empower both the child and the behavior. In response, a child may lose the motivation to modify his behavior. Parents fare better when they develop light-hearted, creative responses that address the child's behavior. Often, a good rule of thumb is "less is more."

> ***Mom:*** *"Allison, let's go to the mall."*
>
> ***Allison:*** *"Why?"*
>
> ***Mom:*** *"I want to buy you something."*
>
> ***Allison:*** *"You do? What?"*
>
> ***Mom:*** *"New ears."*
>
> ***Allison:*** *"New ears?"*
>
> ***Mom:*** *"Yes. The ones you have don't work. I've asked you to pick up your clothes five times and they're still there."*

When parents ask me to name a good parenting role model, they're often surprised when I suggest the television detective Columbo. The beauty of Columbo's style is that he is smart enough to know when to play dumb. He lulls criminals into a false sense of security that ultimately results in their being held accountable for their actions. Substitute the word kids for criminals and you should get the picture. How can you as a parent learn from the police force how to better enforce rules at home? Picture the diminutive, slovenly dressed Columbo as the dad in the following illustration.

Dad: "Son, I owe you an apology."

Bruce: "Why, Dad?"

Dad: "Because I thought going to the movies with your friends this weekend was really important. I was wrong and I apologize."

Bruce: "But Dad. I can't wait to go."

Dad: "Thanks for trying to make me feel better, son. You're a terrific kid. But we both know that if it was really important to you, you would have finished that school report and cleaned up your room."

Highlighting the consequences of your children's behavior by adopting an apologetic, dumbfounded stance can provide dramatic results. It shifts the burden of responsibility onto your children to police their own actions. This helps them learn to more adeptly anticipate the consequences of their actions and make choices that will heighten their enjoyment and freedom. You must be willing to put on a convincing performance when the curtain goes up. I'm not suggesting you be disingenuous or manipulative. You truly believe in the message you are delivering. Just as children often "act" like they don't care about something important, parents must sometimes allow themselves artistic freedom when fulfilling their parenting role.

Here are a few Columbo-isms for you to fill in the blank:

"I just can't figure out why . . . ."

"There's only one thing that escapes me. Why . . . ."

"So, you don't care if . . . ."

"I'll take someone else if you want, but I'll really miss . . . ."

"Who would have believed that (your child's name) would rather . . . ."

If you choose to add a little drama to your parenting style, consider what George Burns said when asked, "If you had to choose one thing that was most important to your success, what would it be?" He thought for a moment and replied, "If I had to choose one thing, I'd probably say sincerity. Once you learn to fake that, you've got it made."

Ask—Don't Tell

As parents' energy levels diminish, so do their creative resources. The price paid by the entire family is strained communication and alienation, as winless battles are repeatedly waged between incensed parents and tuned out kids. A quick and effective remedy is for parents to switch from a "telling" to an "asking" mode. Virtually any parent directive can be reframed as a thought-provoking question. This tactic helps place the burden of responsibility on children to make wise and acceptable choices about their behavior. In effect, they learn to anticipate and weigh the consequences of their actions before they create conflict.

Again, let's briefly consider the issue of toys. Instead of repeatedly imploring your children to "please pick up your toys now," try posing the following questions:

"What do I need you to do right now?"

"What do you think will happen if you continue to ignore me?"

"What am I thinking right now?"

"What could you do to make me happy right now?"

"Are you going to be a good helper today?"

While calmly asking these questions, try alternating furtive glances between your children and the toys to make it easier for them to read your mind. When they finally "get it," praise their **mind-reading** abilities at the same time you thank them for being cooperative. Next time, simply saying, "Let's play the mind-reader game," may be all you need to short-circuit their resistance.

Like most kids, my daughter Jana becomes a statue in front of the television, and her eyes and ears cease to receive any information that does not come from an animated character. I have proof her senses still work because every day she provides me with a list of the most recent toll-free numbers from which to order the latest advertised toys. I discovered a magical question that helps gain her cooperation virtually every time. I simply ask, "Do you need me to turn off the television to help you listen? I will if you want me to!"

If it becomes necessary to adopt a little harder line with a resistant child, consider experimenting with a more "high-tech" approach. Computer users are quite familiar with the point-and-click method when utilizing a mouse. When your child fails to receive your "sent messages." try reversing the mouse process. Simply "click" (snap your fingers), and then "point" to the target issue (e.g. toys) and/or your child as needed. Then state your position clearly with a simple proclamation such as "I'm finished repeating myself" or "I need your help right now." This should help your kids shift from neutral gear into drive.

I can't over-emphasize how critical the "ask-don't tell" tactic is in creating healthy communication and reducing stress. While it will likely require some retraining and modification of your current style, the dividends are well worth the energy investment. Otherwise, you will start to sound like your parents when you repeatedly exhort, "I'm tired of sounding like a broken record!" And if you're lucky to get any response at all, it's likely to be "Mom, what's a record?"

Pretzel Logic

To develop your own effective creative and humorous techniques, you must stretch the limits of your imagination. One way to enhance your powers of perception and imagination is to learn to see things not simply for what they are — but also for what they can become. Every object, experience or person you encounter can become a catalyst for enriching your interactions with your children. One way to grease your humor wheels is to practice making humorous associations and connections between what you see and the messages you wish to convey. For example, if your child is refusing to listen or arguing with you while eating a pretzel, you might respond, "You twist my words like that pretzel." Registering pictures in your mind and using them as a springboard for your ideas and words can help you open up a vast universe of helpful associations. When you plant in your child's mind common pictures with new meanings, you provide a new stimulus that you can use to remind him of an issue and behavior. Consider the word "pear." You probably envision a fruit, or perhaps a pair of aces, which might make you then picture two top gun pilots who also are aces . . . The point is that you can be as creative as you train yourself to be.

> **Mom:** *"See this pear. It reminds me of you two."*

> **Sisters:** *"Why's that, Mom?"*

> **Mom:** *"Because when I ask you to help me clear the dinner dishes, the two of you pair up and disappear."*

Even if your talents don't lie in spontaneously making up jokes or plays on words, an occasional attempt can energize you and stimulate novel ways for you and your child to relate.

❀ ❀ ❀ ❀ ❀ ❀
"Columbo is smart enough to know when to play dumb."
❀ ❀ ❀ ❀ ❀ ❀

Attention-grabbing techniques can be effective because children are caught off-guard by a mysteriously challenging question. Parents avoid offering harsh criticism without sacrificing the power of the message. The more you are willing to playfully free associate with your everyday surroundings, the more diverse your parenting tool box will become. Instead of your child quickly tuning you out, he will be more likely to utter those four magical words, "What do you mean?" That is music to every parents ears.

When Opportunity Knock-Knocks

You don't have to wait for opportunities to knock when you want to parent creatively. You can create learning opportunities. For example, we all know that choosing clothes is an important form of self-expression and helps shape our identities, even at a very young age. I was amazed that by the time my daughter was 20 months old, she insisted on choosing her clothes each day. Her choice was somewhat predictable, since it was always the one not made by me. Unless my memory fails me, her first words were "Daddy," "Mommy," and "It doesn't match."

No doubt parents and children have been battling about what to wear since the invention of the loincloth. Most parents' first priority is to protect their children from the elements. We also try to teach them how to dress fashionably. Because a child's priorities usually are reversed, parents often are forced to participate in "the clothing wars." Consider this typical battle scene between eight-year-old Eddie and his mother.

Eddie: "Mom, can I go out and play?"

Mom: "Sure, but please put on your rain gear and don't forget your hat. I heard it might drizzle today."

Eddie: "Mom, I can't go out and play with my cool friends looking like that. They'll make me the poster boy for Nerd of the Year! I won't wear that."

Mom: "Yes you will."

Eddie: "I won't."

Mom: "Will."

Eddie: "I hate you."

Mom: "No you don't."

Eddie: "Do . . . ."
And on and on and on.

Now this may not resolve without a fight, but there is another way to "knock" some sense into him.

>*Mom:* "Knock-knock."

>*Eddie:* "Who's there?"

>*Mom:* "Hotch."

>*Eddie:* "Hotch who?"

>*Mom:* "See, Eddie, you already are catching a cold. Please dress like I asked you to."

A technique as simple as a "knock-knock" joke can lend humor to a situation and help diffuse it. When similar circumstances arise in the future, reviving just the "knock-knock" part of the joke can help douse the flame of conflict. Children may cooperate immediately simply to avoid being subjected to your idea of humor. After the tension is broken, the parent should be open to taking another look at the situation and lay the groundwork to solve it jointly.

>*Mom:* "Look, Eddie. I would like you to wear something waterproof. Any suggestions?"

>*Eddie:* "How about my windbreaker. It even has a hood."

>*Mom:* "But that by itself isn't warm enough."

>*Eddie:* "How about if I wear a couple of layers of warm clothing, like my T-shirt and a sweater underneath it?"

>*Mom:* "I think I can live with that. But if I see you getting soaking wet, can you live with me asking you to come in?"

Eddie: "I think so."

Mom: "Okay, let's try it."

Using jokes or other light-hearted responses allows families to put into perspective situations that otherwise might become inflammatory. For example, homework is important, but screaming and yelling seldom lead to cooperation and could lead to passive-aggressive and/or defiant responses. Here's another way.

Mom: "Knock-knock."

Carla: "Not again. Okay. Who's there?"

Mom: "Butter."

Carla: "Butter who?"

Mom: "Butter go finish your homework if you want to watch your favorite show tonight."

Try these three, which also have universal application:

Dad: "Knock-knock."

Carla: "Who's there?"

Dad: "Olive."

Carla: "Olive, who?"

Dad: "Olive a lot longer if you would . . . ."

Mom: "Knock-knock."

Evan: *"Who's there?"*

Mom: *"Anita."*

Evan: *"Anita, who?"*

Mom: *"Anita little help around here."*

* * * * * *

Dad: *"Knock-knock."*

Brian: *"Who's there?"*

Dad: *"Ya."*

Brian: *"Ya who?"*

Dad: *"I knew you'd be excited about taking out the garbage."*

One mother complained to me about how her son ignores her. Despite repeatedly telling him, "You act as if I'm not even here," little had changed. Then she tried a new tactic.

Mom: *"Knock-knock."*

Bruce: *"Who's there?"*

Mom: *"You tell me!"*

Most of my knock-knock techniques are designed to elicit a light-hearted response from your child, which might facilitate constructive communication. But most parents admit that sometimes they don't want to hear even another syllable from their child, especially when he is driving them crazy. I have developed one foolproof technique that virtually ensures momentary silence from your child. Unfortunately, it usually only works once. But as the saying goes, "enjoy it while it lasts." Here it is:

> **Mom:** "Hal, you certainly have an answer for everything, don't you."
>
> **Hal:** "If you say so."
>
> **Mom:** "Well, I'm tired of arguing with you. By the way, I heard a funny joke today. Want to hear it?"
>
> **Hal:** "Sure."
>
> **Mom:** "Okay, you say knock-knock."
>
> **Hal:** "Knock-knock."
>
> **Mom:** "Who's there?"
>
> **Hal:** " . . . . "
> (Savor your victory and brief moment of silence!)

Consider the use of another classic set-up, which can be used in different ways when opportunities arise.

> **Mother:** "Tommy, what do you get when you cross a boy and a bicycle?"
>
> **Tommy:** "I don't know. What?"
>
> **Mother:** " A boy who is always late for dinner. What don't you get the next time you cross the same boy with the same bicycle?"
>
> **Tommy:** "I'm afraid to ask. What?"
>
> **Mother:** "Dessert!"

Virtually any two commonly linked, but competing activites can be presented this way:

> **Mom:** *"Susan, what do you get when you cross a TV with homework?"*
>
> **Susan:** *"Uh oh. What?"*
>
> **Mom:** *"A daughter who would rather do homework on the weekend than go to a movie."*
>
> **Susan:** *"Four score and seven years ago . . ."*

What I have illustrated here is that familiar jokes can be adapted in novel ways to communicate and negotiate with your children. All around us are familiar objects, sayings, situations and behaviors that we can modify or reinterpret to lessen the tensions between parents and children. You just have to be willing to experiment with creative alternatives to yelling and dictating. Take a few minutes and try to make up a knock-knock joke of your own. Like anything else, using knock-knock or other jokes with your children initially can be challenging and draining. But if you're willing to utilize your creativity, these jokes can reduce fatigue and even improve your adult relationships. Here's how:

> **Wife:** *"Knock-knock."*
>
> **Husband:** *"Who's there?"*
>
> **Wife:** *"Needs a vacation."*
>
> **Husband:** *"Needs a vacation who?"*
>
> **Wife:** *"You and I. Without the kids. As soon as possible."*

Milky Way Bars Can Fly

Raising children provides an endless supply of food for thought. When shopping with your children at the supermarket, it's inevitable that the shopping cart will magically fill with candy as soon as you turn your head to select a nutritious snack. A simple question such as, "When did Milky Ways learn to fly?" often will be as effective as, "Are you out of your mind?" or "You'll never eat another piece of candy as long as you live!"

Consider another common food problem that arises at mealtime. Even the best parent chefs experience frustration trying to prepare meals their children will dare to taste. This often results in a power struggle like the following one between eight-year-old George and his mother.

Mom: "Here's your dinner."

George: "I hate that. I'm not eating it. I want hot dogs."

Mom: "You had hot dogs the last seven nights in a row, and it's not even baseball season. Tonight we're having something different."

George: "I don't care. Besides, it looks like road kill."
Mom: "We're having liver and onions tonight. You've eaten this before. I used Aunt Nettie's recipe."

George: "I'm not eating it tonight, Mom."

Mom: "Then you'll sit at this table until you eat it or turn 21 — whichever comes first."

George: "Okay, but can I leave for a few hours when I'm sixteen to take my driving test?"

Mom: "George, if you ever hope to put the pedal to the metal, then I'd better see you eat a sliver of liver."

Another alternative would be for George's mother to calmly address the issue indirectly the next time he asks to eat dinner at a friend's house.

George: "Mom, Sammy's mother invited me over for dinner tomorrow. Can I go?"

Mom: "Is it important to you?"

George: "Yes!"

Mom: "Okay. You can eat dinner at Sammy's under one condition."

George: "What's that?"

Mom: "When Sammy's mother puts your plate of food in front of you, I want you to say, 'I hate that! I'm not eating it! It looks like roadkill.'"

George: "I can't say that to his mom!"

Mom: "What do you mean? You have no problem saying it to me a few times a week. (Pause.) Listen, it's fine if you want to eat at Sammy's, but for me to say yes, I expect that you will be more cooperative and respectful at our dinner table. Do you get it?"

George: "Yeah. So can I go to Sammy's?"

Mom: "Sure. By the way, Sammy's mother asked me if I would come over tomorrow afternoon and help her make my famous liver and onions for dinner. I told her I'd be delighted, so I'll see you there."

The beauty of this technique — which addresses problem behaviors in the absence of a power struggle — is that it helps create a "parenting web." Unacceptable behaviors that persist become intertwined with other situations and requests that force the child to consider his actions. While parents attempt to teach their children how to behave properly, they also should teach them how to think and make sound decisions. Requests can be granted while getting extra mileage out of them. Using creative tactics can expedite positive behavior changes and promote more of a give-and-take relationship.

"When did Milky Ways learn to fly?"

The technique used by George's mother nicely incorporates the (unexpected) "T" of timing. The issue of how George treats his mother (process) was revisited through an unexpected content (asking to eat at a friend's house). Although dredging up old issues may be labeled unfair by a child, parents can remind them that their unchanged behavior is what keeps the issue alive. Parents can constructively raise unresolved issues by using creativity and humor.

Gary: "Can I play at Boomer's house tomorrow?"

Mom: "I think so. Just tell me how many times you plan to hit Boomer's sister."

Gary: "Are you crazy, Mom?"

Mom: "Am I crazy? You're the one who always hits your sister. Why should Boomer's be any safer? It's only fair that I warn Boomer's mother to stock up on Bandages and ice packs."
(A serious discussion should follow during which Gary clearly understands that his behavior at home will affect the freedom he enjoys outside the home.)

Solutions to Car Wars

Fifty years ago, the highlight of the week for many families was Sunday afternoon, when everyone piled into the Packard with Mom and Dad in the front seat while Buffy, Biff and Princess sat quietly with their hands folded in the rumble seat. In the typical family of the '90s, Cody and Cassidy attempt to claw their way into the front seat of the family's utility vehicle while Kathie Lee yells at them to be quiet so she can hear what Frank is saying on the cellular phone. While I may be guilty of some subtle stereotyping, most readers would agree that in our fast-paced mobile world, parents spend a great deal of time in the car chauffeuring their children. Usually, it is the children who have the busiest schedules.

Once in a blue moon, arguments between children erupt in the car. I realize I might be understating the situation. Perhaps Rodney Dangerfield's famous quip, "I went to the fights the other night and a hockey game broke out" serves as a realistic analogy of how often siblings fight in the car. So how should parents handle arguments in the car? If you own a limousine, I suggest you sit in the front seat and roll up the soundproof window that separates you from your children in the back. If you don't own a limousine, I suggest you look into purchasing or leasing one. If this is not feasible, you may want to invent a remote-controlled electric wall that splits the back seat down the middle. If you have some crazy notion that you would rather rely on your parenting skills than technology, consider some of these techniques that parents have found useful.

> Janet gradually turns up the radio volume when her children fight in the car. It usually is effective in getting their attention, especially if the radio is tuned to a talk radio station. When they complain and ask her to turn it down, she replies, "I'll turn it down when the two of you turn it down." I must caution that if you experiment with this technique, first take note of what is playing on the radio. The ploy may not work if a song such as "Hit Me With Your Best Shot" suddenly blares out of the speakers. You might get pulled over by the police for causing a riot in your car. It is unlikely he'll buy the explanation, "Officer, I was just trying to calm them down."

One common, but rarely successful technique is for parents to threaten to pull to the side of the road. Kids know that this usually is an idle threat. Why would any sane parent whose kids are driving them crazy decide the solution is to pull over and spend more time in the car with them? The problem with pulling to the side of the road is — then what? Whether you stop the car or continue driving, one suggestion is to hold a discussion such as the one below:

Parent: "Do you guys think it's fair what you're doing to me?" (Now they are on the same team instead of fighting against each other.)

Children: "We're not doing anything to you!"

Parent: "Yes you are, and I am very upset with both of you!"

Children: "What are we doing?"

Parent: "You are both fighting, ignoring my requests to stop, and it is very unpleasant for me to be in the car with two kids who choose not to care about me or control themselves." (There is nothing wrong with sometimes turning a car trip into a guilt trip.)

Child: "But he started it!"

Parent: "By saying that, you are the one who is keeping it going. Besides, I don't care who started it. I want to know who is going to be first to stop it. Do you (child one) think this is fair? Do you (child 2) think this is fair?"

Children: "No. No."

Parent: "I am glad you are both brave enough to admit you're being unfair. I appreciate your honesty. Now let's decide together how we all can enjoy the rest of the ride."

The key to this discussion is to remain relatively calm but firm while you get your children's attention. Next, ask direct questions that require verbal answers and conclude the discussion only after they agree to behave.

> *When Evelyn's children were fighting in the car, she surprised them by playing "Simon Says." After a few rounds she said, "Simon says cover your mouth with your hands, left hand over right." That was the last command Simon gave. Although her children only fell for this once, Simon Says became their "warning," which usually provoked some laughter as they recalled the first time they were duped into playing it.*

If your children's behavior in the car is driving your crazy, more drastic actions may be required. Kids will know you really mean business if you choose to forego a pleasurable activity and inform them, "I'm sorry, but I just don't want to take the chance of you two fighting and ruining the day for everybody." Put the shared responsibility on them by saying, "When you two figure out a foolproof way to avoid fighting, let me know."

Although I have suggested techniques that may help broker a truce at 60 mph, I can assure you that none of them work all the time. Despite your best efforts, sibling rivalry will exist and persist. While you can prepare yourself to react calmly and cleverly, the next time a World Wrestling Federation championship match occurs in your car, you might react by screaming at the top of your lungs. It may even work. If not, you still can attempt to calmly and creatively referee. I would encourage you to develop your own interventions that reflect the personalities in your family. Perhaps there is a favorite car game you can play to keep them occupied, such as who can make up the funniest name for a person using the letters of a license plate. It's pretty hard for kids not to laugh after spotting Mr. <u>U</u>mus <u>B</u>. <u>N</u>uts making a right turn while his left blinker flashes.

It is important for parents to develop a large and diverse repertoire. Developing patience and maintaining your composure are prerequisites to resolving conflicts with your children. Remember, your kids usually are watching you from the back seat and are likely to model what they observe. So the next time some jerk cuts you off on the highway, for the sake of your kids wouldn't you rather respond, "Kids, Simon must have told that guy to close his eyes," instead of, "You **!!!****!!!"

You're Odd — I'm Even

Sharing is a major dilemma for children, who fear they will lose a competitive edge. A cousin of mine shared a clever parenting tool called the odd-even technique. When siblings fight about crucial world-shaping events such as which cartoon to watch or who bathes first, parents can rely on the calendar to solve these disputes. When two children are involved, one gets to make certain decisions on the odd and the other on even days. Parents should identify which issues and disagreements will be settled this way. Parents can help remove the burden of making a decision by using the odd-even technique. Parents must monitor their children's interactions, however. If you overhear one child say something like, "It's my day, so I get your allowance, too," then a quick clarification of the boundaries will be needed.

After the system is in place, you should explain to each of your children how important it is to find opportunities to "share your power" with their siblings by allowing them to make some choices even when it's your day. This lays the groundwork for them to learn that sometimes "what goes around, comes around." You can intervene at opportune moments to point out when such opportunities to share arise. The concept of reciprocity or paying back a nice deed with another nice gesture often can be better understood and applied when a child feels that the majority of his power is preserved and remains under his control. If you have more than two children, this intervention can be more difficult to implement. One way is to just rotate "control days" between each child.

On your Kids, Get Set, Go!

When parents can use creativity to make a mundane task fun, children are more likely to cooperate. One day, while cleaning out my garage, I discovered an old, forgotten stopwatch. When I explained its purpose to my daughter, she became fascinated with the concept. She insisted I time her running from one end of the yard to the other. The next hour was spent helping her try to break her speed record.

The next day, when she was resisting cleaning up her toys, I spied the stopwatch on the table. Here is what followed:

> **Dad:** *"Are you ready?"*
>
> **Jana:** *"For what?"*
>
> **Dad:** *"To set a new record."*
>
> **Jana:** *"What do you mean?"*
>
> **Dad:** *"I wonder how quickly you can put your toys away."*
>
> **Jana:** *"OK."*
>
> **Dad:** *"On your Jana, get set, go!"*

I sat in a chair while precious seconds ticked away, watching Jana fervently put each toy in its place. I discovered that instead of always yelling for her to clean up, I could simply employ the stopwatch to get her to do as I asked. It was great to realize that I wasn't the only one who appreciated that time is of the essence.

I'll Flip You For It

A friend of mine built a successful sporting goods business by using his creativity. One day in his store, I observed a customer negotiating the price of a pair of skis with a salesman. They remained $80 apart. My friend the owner overheard the conversation and interceded by saying, "I'll flip you for it. Heads, it's my price. Tails, it's yours." This was a great way to break the deadlock, because it removed the tension and replaced it with excitement and intrigue. My friend flipped a coin, the customer made his choice — and lost. The owner responded, "Maybe next time."

Despite having lost the coin toss, a seed was planted that would encourage the customer to return and purchase goods from him in the future. Both participants were prepared to lose because they both had an equal chance to win. Even the "loser" left with a smile on his face.

The implications for parent-child conflicts are obvious. Parents must be flexible and playful in their approach to parenting. Intrigue can help combat fatigue. But it's important to be sure to play fair. Using a two-headed coin is not advisable. (See later section on trust.) If your child insists on always using his coin, offer to shine it up first so you can be sure George Washington doesn't grace both sides. And finally, if your son agrees to this technique with the stipulation, "OK, heads I win, tails you lose," good luck when he becomes a teenager!

Life is a game of chance. Even when we feel cast adrift in a sea of uncertainty, we attempt to influence decisions and situations by acting in ways we hope will lead to a desirable outcome. My creative parenting solutions to parenting dilemmas may leave you thinking, "I can't do that."

Yes, you can.

Every parent can experiment with different problem-solving approaches. If you are willing to "step outside the box" and interact more creatively and playfully, life will be easier and more enjoyable for all.

❋ ❋ ❋ ❋ ❋ ❋
"Intrigue can help combat fatigue."
❋ ❋ ❋ ❋ ❋ ❋

❋ ❋ ❋ ❋ ❋ ❋

Thus far we have examined in depth the Ts of timing and tact. Except in families that have taken a vow of silence, the majority of parental discipline and expectations are communicated verbally. Families who hope to resolve their differences in ways that don't jeopardize the collective joy they experience must become aware of the emotional overtones inherent in how they communicate. Let's now explore the role of tone in raising children.

Don't Drown in the Car Pool!

Tone

CHAPTER SIX

How Do You Sound?

The physical characteristics of a voice and the emotional states of both the speaker and listener combine to shape the perception of someone's tone of voice. Research studies show that one's choice of words isn't the overriding factor that influences how a message is perceived by a listener. Often, more subtle determinants such as tone of voice and body language will determine the quality of the interaction.

What are your reactions to the phrases: "Don't talk to me in that tone of voice." "How dare you talk to me that way." "Who do you think you're talking to?" Chances are, just reading these phrases causes you some discomfort. Someone's tone of voice and the overall tenor of a discussion can greatly affect family life. Although we all have innate vocal qualities and temperaments that influence how we sound and respond to others, we learn through our experiences and role models how to talk, listen, disagree and compromise. Some of us are exposed to better teachers and others of us are better students. Successful communication with children often hinges as much on a child's perception of a parent's tone of voice as it does on objective measures such as frequency and decibel level (although both definitely influence perception). A child who perceives his parent's tone of voice as angry, intimidating or threatening is likely to be

Don't Drown in the Car Pool!

reluctant to engage in conversation. Conversely, vocal tone that conveys indecisiveness, passivity or guilt may encourage a child to exploit a parent's vulnerabilities. Before looking at the role of tone in the daily life of families, let's briefly review some technical terms associated with this phenomenon.

TONE (Signal)	
Physical characteristics of sound	Psychological interpretation
1. Frequency	Pitch
2. Intensity	Loudness
3. Complexity	Quality
4. Length	Duration

Every time we speak, our audible speech primarily is shaped by the variables listed above. The perception of each variable and overall speech is interpreted differently by each speaker and listener. This complex verbal/emotional interaction between speaker and listener impacts how people behave toward one another. Someone's perception of how she is treated is influenced greatly by how she feels when someone speaks to her. Fluctuations in any or all of these variables can result in a person's voice being perceived as "hostile," "loving," "critical," "accepting," and the like. Parents constantly vary the frequency and intensity of their speech in response to their children's actions. Often, they aren't aware of the extent to which they modify their tone of voice. When parents become angry, they often will talk loudly (or yell) in a higher pitched voice. They may increase the duration or length of their words for effect, such as, "Suuusaaan — What are you doing?" Children immediately process and respond to this "angry tone" and, as a result, the tension level in the relationship is heightened and everyone becomes more defensive. Yelling can help children ask important questions like, "What did I do?" or "Why are you blaming me?" (even if blame hasn't been directly assigned). They also make critical judgments about the situation and defend their behavior, such as, "She's making a big deal

94

out of nothing," or "I didn't do anything wrong." Constructive questions can be triggered simply by a parent altering her speech pattern just slightly enough to evoke an emotional reaction from her child. Slightly raising the intensity or pitch can increase cooperation without heightening defensiveness and resentment.

It's also important for parents to become aware of and monitor their breathing patterns. They can have a significant impact on how one's tone of voice is perceived. Breath sounds such as "Sheeesh," "huhhh . . .," or "ahhh," just to highlight a few, create emotional overtones that can dramatically affect the verbal and nonverbal aspects of parent-child interactions.

Although simultaneous changes in body language can affect the impact of a change in tone (furrowed brow, clenched teeth, etc.), tone has a powerful presence even without visual enhancement. Blind people, who often experience a heightening of senses, including hearing, can be more acutely aware than sighted people of the emotional nuances inherent in speech.

We first interpret changes in tone on a physical level. Tightened muscles or closed eyes are common reactions to being yelled at. Some combination of retaliatory actions, thoughts and/or words often will immediately accompany the physical changes. If you are being praised, your body is more likely to relax, expressed through a smile and perhaps some verbal expression of gratitude. Although tone is a physical entity, we constantly interpret changes in tone to help us define the psychological aspects of our world. The more adept parents become at identifying their own and their children's tonal shifts, the greater their influence and interpretive powers become. This is especially important for parents who are experiencing difficulty "reading" a child who may be especially quiet and sensitive. Such children will offer fewer vocal clues to help their parents differentiate sadness from anger, for example. How parents speak to their child during sensitive moments will impact greatly whether the child feels comfortable enough to "open up" and say more about what he's feeling.

Just as tonal variation can convey disapproval, a parent can convey love, acceptance, and amusement by varying the tone of his voice. If the pitch of your voice increases as you speak, you may heighten feelings of tension and distress. Gradually lowering the tone can be soothing and facilitate more open communication. Talking to a misbehaving child with a direct but soothing tone of voice can bring surprisingly positive results. Parents who vary their vocal responses will increase their child's attentiveness and responsiveness.

But for any emotions and responsiveness to be conveyed effectively to children, parents must be perceived as genuine and sincere. Children are adept at spotting phonies. For example, a parent who grits his teeth and mumbles, "I'm really proud of you" isn't likely to boost his child's self-esteem. An angry parent who softly pleads, "Please don't do that again" easily will be dismissed. The tone of a message must be consistent with the content. As parents identify the messages they wish to convey to their children, they must learn to momentarily become the child to experience how their tone is likely to be perceived. If a parent's voice mimics an air raid siren, her children may run for cover and hide (making it even more difficult to talk to them). If the situation escalates, all may need to be rescued by someone who can begin to teach them how to calmly and effectively communicate.

A Mouse Tale

Everyone's temperament is unique. Some people are naturally more irritable, while others appear to cope with life's pressures more easily. During stressful moments we often are unaware of how we come across to others and how seemingly minor gestures or tonal changes in our voice can have significant negative consequences.

While in the final stages of building my house, I allowed a carpenter to continue his work while I was out of town. When I returned, I discovered that a little glass mouse with a tail made from a spring was missing. This mouse had significant sentimental value. It later was discovered in a curio box with the tail almost completely stretched out. I doubted that this was a malicious and premeditated attack. Nor did I suspect it was the handiwork of the handyman. I wondered if perhaps his children accompanied him to work. This put me in a sensitive predicament because I had developed a trusting relationship with the carpenter, whom I was about to accuse of raising children who abuse fragile glass animals.

"Parents must be perceived as genuine and sincere."

The next time I saw him, I casually asked whether his children had been at my home. He seemed surprised at the question, but said his son had been present one day. When I explained what had happened to the tail of the mouse, he promised to question his son regarding his possible role in the caper. I assured him I had no immediate plans to contact the CIA, FBI, or ASPCA. I just wanted to know if this was the work of a lone assassin or a conspiracy.

When the carpenter returned a few days later, he sheepishly reported that his son admitted to having stretched the tail despite earlier having stretched the truth. When he expressed his upset to his son for hiding his mistake, the six-year-old pulled out the heavy artillery.

He said, "Dad, when you work you usually get so frustrated, angry and curse so much that I was afraid to tell you what I accidentally did to the mouse. You raise your voice and then take it out on me. You sound like every little thing I do annoys you. I even feel like your mistakes are my fault. Even though I was playing with the mouse and didn't intend to harm it, I was afraid you would yell and punish me."

As the father related this conversation to me, his eyes took on a "little boy" look, expressing recognition that his low frustration tolerance and angry tone of voice virtually forced his son to hide the mouse. I was impressed by his admission that he needed to "own some of this." He realized that for his son to be honest, he needed to create a comfortable, safe and forgiving atmosphere for him. He recognized that learning to monitor and modify his tone of voice was a key factor in making this change.

Although I never met his son, I was left with the sense that this father-son relationship probably was enhanced by the case of the wounded mouse. As for the mouse, the father arranged for a tail transplant by a jeweler friend and, as far as I know, father, son and mouse have recovered nicely.

Old Yeller

As we saw in a mouse tale, a harsh, intimidating tone can prevent even the most well-intentioned parent from developing an honest, open relationship with his child. Just responding in a hostile tone can be destructive, especially if it dominates a parent's style. It also can have the opposite effect of empowering a child rather than promoting compliance. If a parent can tolerate a child's behaviors long enough to think rationally, she can choose a more effective tone of voice while posing more constructive questions.

Consider the following interaction that occurred between a mother and her nine-year-old son, Michael. Earlier in their treatment with me, I identified a pattern whereby Michael frequently provoked his mother. His mother then would become irate and invest tremendous time and energy in trying to control Michael, often at the expense of attending to the needs of her other children. Michael seemed to enjoy this "special attention," even though it was laced with anger. He privately admitted to me that he believed he had his mother wrapped around his little finger. As his mother gained insight into the problem, she began modifying her tone and interacting in calmer, more effective ways. After much work, the following exchange occurred in my office, which eventually typified how mother learned to react to Michael.

> ***Mother:*** *(in a soft, calm voice) "Michael, I asked you not to throw the ball in the house this morning. Why did you choose to ignore me?"*
>
> ***Michael:*** *"I was just throwing it in the air and catching it. I didn't think anything would happen."*
>
> ***Mother:*** *"Well, you were wrong because now my favorite vase is broken. You also didn't keep your promise only to throw the ball outside. You're promises are important to me and I've always had the impression they were important to you."*
>
> ***Michael:*** *"I'm sorry, Mom. I didn't mean for anything to happen."*
>
> ***Mother:*** *"I am upset about the broken vase, but more upset about the broken promise. I would prefer not to yell at you but to discuss what happened. I hope that you don't need me to yell at the top of my lungs for you to learn a lesson. Do you?"*

Michael: "No. But I expected you to yell. I knew you would be upset."

Mother: "I felt like yelling just like you felt like throwing the ball, but I've learned to control myself."

Michael: "I'll try to control myself, too. I promise."

Many parents think if they don't yell, their children won't take them seriously. Sometimes, this is true. Generally, I have found that yelling isn't the optimal way to promote family harmony. A parent who decides to switch to a consistently calmer tone must allow time for the change to sink in. Although a child may test to see if the calmer tone is a sign of weakness, parents often can be highly effective through the strength of their actions. Parents should experiment with varying the tone of their voices to provide them with options. A parent who feels she has run out of options often is left with no choice but to yell. When anger and yelling pervade, many other positive aspects of a parent-child relationship can be overshadowed or lost.

Making a Bad Situation Worse

Becoming aware of and strategically controlling the tone of one's voice is difficult even under the usual circumstances. But when an unexpected event or tragedy occurs, people may become more ill-tempered and respond accordingly. When a parent loses a helpmate through divorce, illness or death, the burden can be overwhelming. She may become less tolerant, respond to her children in an unduly harsh manner and convey destructive messages she truly regrets sending. People often are unaware that such a shift has occurred.

I once treated a depressed girl I'll call Sarah. Sarah was referred to me six months after the sudden death of her father in an automobile accident. Her father was described as a loving but stern disciplinarian. Her mother, who had a thriving career as an attorney, was left alone with three daughters, ages 2, 4, and Sarah, age 6. The stress of the recent tragedy had caused Sarah's mother to become increasingly irritable and depressed. Sarah gradually became more withdrawn and isolated, and often cried herself to sleep. Other times she would become irritable (like her mother), stubborn and oppositional. During the first session in my office, Sarah spotted my candy jar and began playing "Halloween" by stuffing her pockets with candy. Her mother was embarrassed and responded by yelling, "Sarah, put that candy back. You're a bad girl! Bad girl!" Sarah did as she was told, returned to her chair with a sullen expression and refused to talk the remainder of the session.

As the treatment progressed and I got to know Sarah's mother better, she tearily revealed that she frequently yelled at her children and told them they were "bad." This behavior emerged following the death of her husband. The more adventurous Sarah bore the brunt of it. We discussed other ways she could express her disapproval of their behavior while avoiding personal insults. She also acknowledged the importance of dealing with her grief. Sarah's mother learned to say, "I need your help," or "Right now your behavior is unacceptable. Please do as I ask." After months of hard work, the atmosphere of the home gradually brightened as the anger and tension diminished. Mother became acutely aware of what she said and how she said it.

By dramatically lowering the decibel level and pitch of her voice when disciplining her children, she fostered a cooperative spirit and allowed her family to grieve collectively instead of separately. After she had gained the necessary self-control, she became more playful and creative with her children, even when disciplining them. The following example occurred in my office toward the end of treatment:

Sarah was spinning around in her chair, ignoring her mother's requests for her to stop. Admirably, the mother addressed Sarah by saying in a soft, squeaky voice, "I'm sorry, Pocahontas, but Sarah won't be able to watch you tonight. She decided to ignore me and spin in her chair instead."

That said, Sarah's chair suddenly ran out of gas.

The Impersonation Game

As parents know all too well, children would rather play than work. Smart parents look for opportunities to creatively teach their children in playful ways. Because it is difficult to be creative during stressful moments, parents must step outside themselves to assess the situation more objectively. One way to cultivate and refine your ability to use humor is to play what I call "The Impersonation Game."

The impersonation game requires you to adopt characters with whom your children are familiar. If you recall Sarah's mother, her apology to Pocahontas for her daughter's behavior was spoken in character to gain her daughter's attention and cooperation. Disney and Sesame Street characters are timeless, although en vogue characters also can be effective. To promote cooperation in younger children, a parent might ask, "What would Big Bird ask you to do if he saw your toys all over?" For older children, borrowing the persona of a current T.V. or movie character can be useful. It doesn't matter if the impersonation is bad. Sometimes, the worse it is, the better.

Mom: (in character voice) "Steven, it's time to round up the crew for dinner. Tell everybody to leave their phasers outside."

Steven: "Who is that supposed to be, Mom?"

Mom: "Captain Kirk of the Starship Enterprise. You love that old show. Pretty good, huh?"

Steven: "Please stop talking like him. I can't take it. You sound more like Elmo from Sesame Street."

Mom: "I can't help it. Captain Kirk just took over my body. He said he won't leave until everyone's seated at the table. Emergency! Emergency! Everybody at the table now! This is your captain speaking!"

In addition to borrowing favorite character voices, parents can use songs to help their children tune into their requests. Kids need not be familiar with a song for this strategy to work. I was told the following vignette by a magazine writer:

> The writer was visiting a friend we'll call Jody, who had been lamenting her lack of creativity as a parent. While there, an argument broke out between Jody and her five-year-old son, who had barely touched his lunch. Suddenly, Jody launched into her own rendition of the song, "Hey, Big Spender," only she changed the words to, "Hey, Big Eater, eat a little more for me." Her son smiled and began eating. The irony was that she didn't realize just how spontaneously creative she had been.

These exercises may seem a bit silly to some of you. You also may have trouble envisioning yourself feeling comfortable participating in them. If so, that's all the more reason to try. Remember, your home isn't a corporate board office or a court of law. It is a place where adults and children attempt to have fun living together. Your time with your children is both precious and fleeting. If you can loosen up enough to pretend you're in charge of a fleet of starships, you are more likely to gain better command of your home base.

* * * * * *

To summarize, tone is an important part of the communication process between parents and children. Parents can creatively alter their tone to elicit cooperation and model more appropriate ways to converse. Children scrutinize their parents to learn acceptable ways to respond to people and situations. To yell at your children, "Don't you yell at me," isn't likely to lead to the results you desire. Even subtle changes in tone can have a dramatic effect. Playfully borrowing the voices of others can reduce tension and increase cooperation. Changing a familiar melody can promote family harmony.

Because parenting is a stressful endeavor, we tend to react quickly and emotionally to our children. Parents must learn to listen to their own tone of voice, just as a mechanic listens closely to an engine's idle. Just because it makes noise, doesn't mean it's working well. Since a parent's voice often is her primary communication vehicle, it occasionally will require fine-tuning to avoid a communication breakdown.

Don't Drown in the Car Pool!

Tolerance

CHAPTER SEVEN

I've Had it Up to Here!

"I'm mad as hell and I'm not gonna take it any more."

You may remember this famous scene from the movie *Network,* where Peter Finch shouts to the world from his office window that he has reached his tolerance limit. How prophetic these words were, since he died shortly after the movie was released and received a posthumous Oscar for Best Actor.

Unfortunately, for the average person starring in the parent role, public awards are far and few between. Wouldn't it be nice if one day you received a call telling you that you are being nominated by the American Academy of Pediatrics for best performance of self-control during a three-year-old's temper tantrum? And if you win, you could then triple your fee for parenting — well, never mind.

So why do parents put forth so much effort day in and night out, engaging in power struggles around such monumental issues as dirty clothes on the floor, watching videos, or developing a precise scientific formula for the number of peas a child must eat to be allowed to stuff his face with cookies?

For centuries, philosophers have tried to explain the underpinnings of human tolerance for the challenges and pressures of everyday existence. A number of timeless expressions have resulted, such as, "What doesn't kill you, makes you strong," (Nietzsche); "If at first you don't succeed, try, try, try again," *(W.E. Hickson);* or, "If at first you don't succeed, pay someone else to do it." *(Berkowitz).*

Many of us have endured experiences that test the limits of our physical and emotional tolerance. Some have even survived unusual and stressful circumstances such as combat, plane crashes, or hailing a cab on a rainy day in New York City. While we often feel exasperated and wonder whether we are capable of surviving such ordeals, upon reflection, most people find that by surviving they have benefited emotionally and become more tolerant of life's pressures.

I have worked with many distraught parents who believed they had reached their limit with their children. Sometimes these parents stated a preference to be stranded alone on a desert island or an isolated mountaintop. At least then they could get some rest and nobody would ask them to take an extra turn in the car pool. However, most parents don't resort to such extremes for a moment's peace. They tend to live day-to-day trying to find a workable balance between the ongoing pressures of parenting and taking care of themselves emotionally and physically.

The issue of tolerance is a complex one. A parent's ability to be patient and flexible varies from moment to moment and situation to situation. Emotional, physical and environmental factors influence one's ability to withstand the onslaught of pressures. Furthermore, parents are not always aware of the degree to which they are being tolerant or intolerant. For this reason, it is important to find some time (and method) for self-examination to understand your limitations. Are you an individual who tends to be reactive and irritable, or are you one who takes things in stride without becoming easily upset and overwhelmed? An individual's inability to tolerate life's pressures is often what draws people to psychotherapy, where they attempt to learn how to more effectively manage their lives.

"Parents are not always aware of the degree to which they are being tolerant or intolerant."

Learning to Talk (and Listen) to Yourself

Talking to yourself sometimes can be an indication that a serious psychological problem exists. When it comes to effective parenting, talking to yourself is an invaluable tool. People constantly talk to themselves, which is why the human race invented meditation exercises to provide relief from the often annoying internal chatter called thought. Whether we are brushing our teeth or designing software for NASA, we talk to ourselves to ensure that we successfully go up and down. Even a mime, who does her act in absolute silence, must talk to herself to give a convincing performance.

Improving one's ability to conduct one-on-self dialogues is at least as important as fine tuning your ability to conduct one-on-one discussions with other people. During moments of intolerance, it often is difficult to think clearly and respond optimally. The more apt you are to analyze and silently rehearse how you will handle difficult situations, the better your chances are of resolving them or avoiding them altogether.

Because of the frenetic pace of society, we often operate on automatic pilot while engaging in fleeting conversations with ourselves. Sometimes, our private dialogues are all that stand between us and a full-fledged anxiety attack. I recently contemplated the implications of this phenomenon while sitting in the forwardmost seat of an airplane. When the flight attendant opened the cockpit door to serve the flight crew lunch, I observed that nobody was flying the plane. The crew casually ate lunch while the plane apparently flew itself. This certainly provided me with a reason to talk to myself. Because a parachute wasn't included with my delicious snack, I decided to give the airline the benefit of the doubt that this was a normal and safe procedure. Talking to myself helped to quell the sudden rise in my anxiety level. Although this might be routine for the crew, I definitely would have felt more secure if I'd heard a crew member ask, "What's our altitude?" instead of "Would you please pass the Grey Poupon?"

If you agree that learning to talk to yourself is valuable, I encourage you to be nice – to yourself as well as to others. You are not at fault if you become upset with something or somebody. You *are* responsible if you need to better manage your upset, yet don't try to do anything about it. Saying to yourself, "Calm down, you jerk" or some other self-deprecating response will only fuel your upset and result in another obstacle for you to overcome. You can get a lot more mileage from phrases like "slow down," "make a choice," or "take a deep breath." If someone else asks you to calm down before you have a chance to catch yourself, it will be to your benefit to respond cordially rather than become upset with them for being right.

Helping Children Cope with Frustration

To help children cope with frustration, parents first must learn to deal with their own. Learning to handle frustration is a lifelong process that includes two phases. The first phase involves learning to identify and manage your reactions and behavior when frustration occurs. Next comes the challenge of containing the frustration long enough to develop and implement constructive responses to aggravating situations. Although avoidance or withdrawal from troublesome situations sometimes is wise, it isn't always feasible or beneficial. A six-year-old child who is frustrated with school, for example, may not solve the problem by dropping out and joining the Peace Corps.

Frustration usually arises suddenly and without warning. Even situations we anticipate can lead to frustration and anger. If poor frustration tolerance is a significant problem and some method of damage control isn't developed, then even minor frustrations can become overwhelming and perpetuate conflict.

A uniquely intense aspect of the parent-child relationship is that the frustration of one usually results in frustration for both. Children often become frustrated because they are struggling to master numerous challenges. Parents often feel helpless and frustrated because children refuse to cooperate or reject their parents' efforts to help them cope.

A person's ability to handle frustration is determined partly by his biological makeup. People described as "high strung" experience greater difficulty coping with frustration and controlling their reactions than those who seem to "roll with the punches." Also, the number of siblings, step-siblings, parents and step-parents can be a significant factor in the frequency and intensity of conflicts leading to anger and frustration. A home's atmosphere (punitive vs. forgiving) plays a major role in the tolerance level of each family member. Being tuned into the atmosphere of your home requires that you monitor what is happening while maintaining an open mind to the opinions of others.

Unusually stressful circumstances also can impact the ability of family members to cope with frustration. These stressors may be on-going or acute, such as a chronic illness or the unexpected death of a loved one. People often have shorter fuses when dealing with crises. Sometimes, people who generally are calm can boil over, even if the heat is only gradually increased.

Many days we awaken knowing that we are not at our best. A crisis may be brewing, or perhaps we just wake up on the wrong side of the futon. Recognizing that this is "just one of those days," and being more sensitive and tolerant of others is much healthier than making everyone else pay for our moodiness. You can turn your quick trigger into ammunition to help others.

Following are two vignettes of families with whom I consulted when their preadolescent daughters had trouble managing their frustration in an age-appropriate manner.

I'd Like to Thank the Academy

Some parents struggle with children who give Emmy-winning performances night after night, yet do not earn enough from their starring roles for lunch money. I recall one parent whose seven-year-old daughter Amy sometimes would threaten to kill herself when she didn't get her way. This mother, who is bright and well educated, often found herself at a loss as to how to respond to her daughter's theatrics.

It became obvious that Amy's goal was to take as much control of her world as possible. She would talk as if she were willing to take desperate measures, and her mother didn't know to what lengths she would go to get her way. When her mother attempted to engage her in constructive discussions about her threats and underlying needs, she encountered significant resistance, increased threats and even temper tantrums.

First, it is important to emphasize that some children are at risk for self-harm. If your child appears significantly depressed, has a history of engaging in high-risk or self-destructive behaviors, or if you just have a gut feeling that she needs professional help, seek appropriate advice.

However, if you are fairly confident that your child doesn't fall into a high-risk category and that you are dealing with a power struggle, your goal should be to help your child learn to tolerate frustration and develop more appropriate coping mechanisms.

Here was my advice to Amy's mother:

- *Remind yourself that Amy's struggle probably is almost as distressing to her as it is to you.* **(EMPATHY)**

- *Tell her that her concerns and needs will be addressed when she is calm enough to engage in a productive discussion.* **(PROCESS)**

- *Don't overreact and risk reenforcing her dramatic and dangerous attention-getting style. Let her know you're prepared to wait until she calms down.* **(TOLERANCE)**

- *Use the child's upsetting and anger-provoking behavior as an opportunity to help her develop a healthier, more appropriate coping style.* **(REFRAMING)**

Previously, Amy's mother became partially immobilized by concern that her daughter might carry out her threats. She became angry at Amy for going to drastic lengths to manipulate her. Sometimes, she would attempt to diffuse the situation and protect Amy from herself by giving in. Other times, she attempted unsuccessfully to ignore her. There always existed this nagging feeling of uneasiness, based on her not being confident that she could trust Amy to maintain good judgment and eventually accept "no" for an answer. Based on our discussions,

Amy's mother learned how to creatively and constructively engage her when threats arose. She calmly responded, "You are obviously upset about something, but by threatening and shouting, you are telling me you are not ready to discuss what you really need. Until you calm down and cease making threats, I cannot talk to you about how I might be able to help."

This response incorporates the four points described above, and provided Amy's mother with a way to respond reasonably and constructively to her daughter's unreasonable behavior. It also defused the power of Amy's threats by labeling them as the obstacle (rather than a vehicle) to get her way. Sometimes, a brief "time-out" was utilized, not as a punishment, but as an opportunity for Amy to calm down while both she and her mother collected their thoughts. After Amy convinced her mother that she was ready to talk about the situation (ah, how the tables turn), her mother first addressed her threats by asking, "What do you expect me to do when you say you want to kill yourself?" When Amy responded, "It's not fair...," the comment allowed for discussion about fairness and whether Amy's threats were fair to her mother. Although the initial conversations were not as productive as later ones, gradually mother and daughter were able to discuss issues of tolerance and trust. Taking care of one another by responding appropriately and safely to frustration became a goal they each could embrace. Also, Amy learned to increase her tolerance for the word "no."

What seemed to strengthen their alliance was Amy's mother's discussions about Amy's current and future requests for increased freedom (such as sleeping over at a friend's house). Amy's mother asked her, "How can I trust you overnight at a friend's when you tell me I shouldn't trust you in our own house?" Amy's mother found herself in a position of strength and was able to help her daughter see that girls who talk (not threaten), are more likely to gain the cooperation and support of their parents. Increased freedom was linked to increased self-control.

One footnote to this vignette is that when a parent introduces a "new" response geared toward redirecting a child's behavior, children will try hard to convince their parents to abandon the new tactic. A temporary increase in the undesirable behavior may occur, signaling that the child is becoming more solidified in her stance. But if a parent is resilient and can weather the storm, most children eventually will adopt healthier behavior patterns.

Post-Traumatic Dress Disorder

Michelle was an attractive nine-year-old girl who was having trouble making decisions. This problem worsened and was frustrating her and her parents. Michelle, like most girls her age, was becoming self-conscious about her image and appearance. Almost daily, the following interaction occurred, as reported to me by her mother. To understand the situation from her mother's perspective, I requested that she give me the following written description:

It is fifteen minutes before the school bus is due. Michelle is still lazing in her pink nightie, her eyes glued to the television, which has become her morning routine.

> "Let's get dressed for school now," her mother suggests, helpfully.
>
> "You have to help me," responds a reluctant Michelle. "I don't know what to wear."
>
> "OK," says her mom. "It's going to be cold today, so here are your leggings, a sweatshirt and a turtleneck."
>
> "No," shouts Michelle. "I don't want to wear that."
>
> "Then how about your blue jeans and your red sweater?" says her mom, trying to maintain her cool.
>
> "No!"
>
> "Your pink warm-up suit?"
>
> "I hate that, Mom!" says Michelle, now screaming.
>
> "Michelle," says the now thoroughly exasperated mom, "How can I help you choose your clothes if you reject everything I suggest? Why don't you just pick out your

own clothes?"

"No, you do it!" responds Michelle.

Back to square one.

Michelle's mom related that as she felt a time limit near, she did her best to help Michelle get dressed for school. She ran into a brick wall of "nos" and became exasperated, intolerant, and overwhelmed because she couldn't identify a strategy that worked. She was developing a case of what I call "Post-Traumatic Dress Disorder." When I asked her what options were available to her, she listed the following:

- *Let Michelle get on the bus in her nightie and be totally humiliated, thus landing Mom in the "Most Hated Hall of Shame."*

- *Wait out Michelle as long as possible, drive her to school late and let her deal with the consequences there.*

- *Switch her to a school requiring uniforms.*

- *Play along until the clothing choices are exhausted with the hope that Michelle will settle on something.*

There is one important difference between the first two and last two options. The first two primarily put the burden of responsibility on Michelle. Mother admitted that she would feel ashamed if she used the first strategy, with such publicly embarrassing consequences. The issue of Mother feeling ashamed if Michelle suffered a consequence brought on by her own behavior was an obstacle that would prevent this or other interventions from being effective. While the second choice also puts pressure on Michelle to consider changing her behavior, the waiting period for Mom likely would feel like self-torture. Also, it was unlikely that Mom could remain neutral and unresponsive to Michelle during this waiting period because Michelle inevitably would become upset and attempt to involve her mother in her struggle.

The third choice of switching to a school requiring a uniform was impractical and didn't address the underlying parent-child dynamics causing the conflict. The final solution of playing along until the clothing choices are exhausted likely would lead to mother becoming exhausted before the clothes.

To find a solution that worked, a careful assessment had to be made of the overall problem. I knew that Michelle was a child who enjoyed being the center of attention and sometimes experienced difficulty when she wasn't. This was most obvious when her parents were talking to other adults and Michelle frequently interrupted with rather arbitrary requests for things that clearly could wait. When she made such requests, she often did so in a babyish voice, accompanied by a somewhat polished "cutesy" presentation. I seldom observed a strong message of disapproval from either parent when Michelle attempted to dominate their attention in this way.

I suggested to her mother that the primary issue was Michelle's need to have control, and if she didn't have it she attempted to create distress in her mother that mimicked her own. Her mother accepted this premise, and realized that for Michelle to continue feeling in control, not making a decision about her clothes was extremely important. After accepting my feedback, Michelle's mother and I agreed on the following intervention.

Mom: *"Michelle, I like the fact that we have some time together in the morning, but I do not enjoy arguing with you about your clothes. I understand that it puts too much pressure on you to watch television before you get dressed. From now on, I will help you by allowing you to watch TV only after you are dressed in your school clothes. After you turn on the television, you cannot change your clothes again."*

Michelle: *"I don't like that idea. I'll get dressed from now on. Besides, on a lot of days, I don't have a problem."*

Mom: *"That is true. But it is a problem for you and me quite often. The answer is not for me to pick out your clothes, but to figure out a way I can help you pick out your own clothes."*

Michelle: *"Please give me a chance. I'll show you!"* *(Michelle continues to fight for control.)*

Mom: *"I know you will be able to do it, but you are not there yet. We will use my plan, which will give you a chance to show me whether you are serious about this (challenge). After you are successful day after day, I promise you another chance to make your own morning schedule."*

This last comment is important in that it gives Michelle a chance to regain some degree of control while re-asserting that Mom maintains overall control. Although it took some time, the balance of power eventually shifted and parent-child boundaries were more clearly established. As you might expect, Michelle sometimes tried to sabotage the new program by regressing in her dressing and other behaviors. To her mother's credit, she stood her ground and remained focused and determined to deal with the underlying power struggle. While learning to avoid power struggles without avoiding the issues, Michelle's mother became less concerned about the hall of shame and ceased becoming a pawn in Michelle's game.

Dress You Up in My Love

Marsha and her five-year-old daughter Caren also were locked in epic battles about what to wear. Like Michelle, she became easily frustrated and rejected her mother's daily fashion input. It was clear to me that Marsha, too, was developing a classic case of Post-Traumatic Dress Disorder. Here is a synopsis of our conversation, which resulted in a creative and effective solution.

Dr. B: "I want you to think outside the box and tell me how you and Caren can narrow her choices."

Marsha: (after considerable thought): "How about if I assign a different color for each day and arrange her closet accordingly. She will have to choose an outfit with that day's color."

Dr. B: "Now you're thinking! By the way, do you have a boom box?"

Marsha: "Yes. Why?"

Dr. B: "How about putting it in her room each day and have her play one song she enjoys. If she doesn't pick out an outfit before the song ends, she must wear the outfit you choose."

Marsha: "Great! I'll try it."

The next week I saw Marsha she literally danced her way into my office. Madonna would have been flattered to hear her sing, *Dress You Up In My Love*. The tactic worked beautifully and helped turn an intolerable routine into fun. She and Caren developed a morning routine of singing, dancing and dressing, often with the entire family joining in.

The Beat Goes On

As we have just seen, creativity sometimes can alter the course of a parent-child power struggle, especially when you're willing to dance to a different drummer. Parenting is like dancing to a song that never ends. Despite exhaustion, you continue to go through the motions, hope for a second and third wind, and pray that you're not making a complete fool of yourself.

Tolerance isn't an issue for parents only during power struggles with children. A family is tested in many ways as they grow together and experience life. Even during pleasurable activities such as vacations, the preparation can be stressful and result in conflict. Trying to convince your son, for example, that he cannot bring a large suitcase full of video games on your spiritual trek through the Himalayas may be no easy task. Parents must expect and be prepared to deal with unexpected and unwanted conflict. While parents often focus on the big picture ("What a great vacation we're going to have!"), a child tends to deal with more immediate concerns ("What's a vacation without Game Boy? I'll never find inner peace!").

Because parents understandably become fatigued and overwhelmed, tolerance sometimes is difficult if not impossible to maintain. But it is better to stay involved with your children and learn together how to become more tolerant rather than withdraw to avoid becoming overwhelmed.

Parents must do some soul-searching to decide how to constructively handle the moments of anguish and frustration that inevitably occur when raising children. Successfully staying in control when angry or frustrated is excellent confirmation that you are mature enough to be a parent even though you still might feel (and sometimes act) like a kid. Kids have no idea how even their simplest requests can drain parents of what little energy they were keeping in reserve. "Mom, I want a peanut butter and jelly sandwich without the crust, lightly toasted and cut into eight pieces. I have to have it on my Rugrats plate. I also want my own Milky Way." You panic momentarily until you realize he is only referring to the candy bar. Such complex demands involving simple tasks understandably annoy parents. But they also can be amusing because they provide parents with a glimpse into their child's imagination. Parents who maintain a sense of humor and are tolerant of minor irritants will find it easier to parent creatively when faced with a variety of challenges.

If parents utilize their maturity and creative resources to set examples of tolerance and self-control, children undoubtedly will take note. Exhibiting a lack of tolerance is likely to elicit the same. Of all the responsibilities handled by parents, perhaps the most important one is how they handle themselves. Children possess the uncanny ability to constantly keep their parents on their toes, even when there's no music playing. Each generation seems to become more skilled at entering their parents into the "for parents only" dance marathon. And the beat goes on.

＊　＊　＊　＊　＊　＊

No matter how closely we monitor our actions and reactions, children present multiple daily challenges that test our composure. Increasing your tolerance level is always a work in progress. Although it is exhausting to constantly monitor your tolerance level, it's impossible to maximize the impact of timing, tact and tone without maintaining a reasonable degree of self-control. Learning to manage your frustration is essential to laying a solid foundation for the final T – **Trust.**

Trust

CHAPTER EIGHT

A Delicate Process

Building trust is a two-way street. Parents must create avenues of opportunity for their children to prove they are trustworthy. This can be an anxiety-provoking process for parents because increased freedom often is necessary to evaluate a child's trustworthiness. Parents engage in an ongoing assessment of a child's judgment and dependability. Parents also must conduct themselves in ways that convince their children that they, too, can be trusted. This involves keeping promises, not betraying secrets and behaving in consistent ways that allow their children to view them as approachable and even as confidants. Children often interpret parental limits as evidence that their parents don't trust them. However, children also trust that their parents will protect them by helping them make sound decisions or, if necessary, by making them for them. Of course, they reserve the right to vehemently protest when parents make unpopular decisions.

So, how does a child develop trust? In part, it involves the children's experience with the previous four Ts (timing, tact, tone and tolerance), which prepare them for the types of parental responses they can expect.

Children learn that certain behaviors will evoke praise, while others will lead to conflict and rebuke. Even when children are surprised by unexpected parental responses, trust usually will endure as long as parents remain relatively consistent in their values and behavior.

Laying the foundation for a trusting parent-child relationship is a delicate process. Children need to trust that their parents accept and love them despite their flaws.

> *Let's say a child is on a baseball team coached by his overly critical father, who yells at him every time he strikes out. He may become more self-critical — view himself as inadequate, and his performance in school even may decline. Low self-esteem may develop and he may experience difficulty trusting others even when they are supportive of him. Many of the seeds of trust or mistrust germinate in parent-child relationships. A child's self-confidence depends greatly on which grows stronger.*

Confidence in one's abilities usually is affected both by objective and subjective feedback. If a child strikes out 20 times in a row, it's hard for him to ignore the objective statistics. If the child gets a hit one out of every three times at bat (.333 batting average), that usually would warrant Hall of Fame consideration in the major leagues. The subjective feedback from his father or coach is equally, if not more powerful. If either one expects him to get a hit every other time at bat (.500 batting average) and berates him for anything less, the child may develop unrealistically high expectations of himself and have trouble trusting peers or other adults who he may anticipate will criticize him harshly. As a way to cope, he may shy away from challenges for fear of failure or embarrassment.

It's unrealistic to expect our children to always obey our wishes, exercise good judgment, choose the "right" friends or follow the right examples. It takes parents and children years to define what constitutes an acceptable level of mutual trust. As a child grows, trust must be reevaluated frequently so appropriate freedoms can be granted.

Parents must create a trust training ground for safe experimentation. When kids are young, every day activities can promote respect and trust.

"Can I trust you will brush your teeth before I come in to say 'good night'?"

"Can I trust that you will put your toys away quickly if I let you play for five more minutes?"

"Can I trust you will practice controlling your anger?"

Inserting the word "trust" in common, everyday communication helps parents and children to develop a mentality of shared responsibility.

Parents trust their children will embrace responsibility, while children trust their parents to provide opportunities to prove they're trustworthy. When using the word trust in the above examples, checking on the outcome is initially important. But as quickly as parents can, they should only spot check as needed. Offering unexpected praise such as, "You really do keep your word," or "Thanks for being such a great helper," enhances trust.

We hope our children will learn from their mistakes (and ours) and will give off discernible verbal and/or behavioral signals when they need guidance. A parent's anxiety grows as the stakes increase because children insist on greater freedom and less supervision. Again, parents can insert the word "trust" in important questions as a way of reminding a child that Mom and Dad are still watching, even if they aren't around.

> *"Can I trust you'll call me right after the movie ends?"*
>
> *"Can I trust you will finish the school project before your Friday sleepover?"*
>
> *"Can I trust you won't get in the car if the driver has consumed any alcohol or drugs?"*

The development of trust also is enhanced when children are included in the decision-making process.

> **Dad:** *"Well, Jim, what do you think your curfew should be?"*
>
> **Jim:** *"How about Thursday? Just kidding. I think midnight is fair."*
>
> **Dad:** *"I'm not quite ready for that. I'd like to start at 11:30."*
>
> **Jim:** *"For how long, Dad?"*
>
> **Dad:** *"That depends on how you handle the 11:30 curfew."*
>
> **Jim:** *"Okay. I'll show you."*
>
> **Dad:** *"To show I have confidence in you and do trust you, I'll make your curfew anytime up to 11:40. I think you're entitled to some flexibility."*

Because child-rearing sometimes feels more like the blind leading the blind (the parent and child taking turns leading), parents are forced to trust their instincts and their children as they follow a natural course toward independence.

As children grow, they often dismiss their parents' input and learn the hard way (which isn't necessarily the wrong way). This can result in a standoff, because parents and children never can be absolutely sure who is in the best position to make decisions in certain situations. Inflexible parents may deny their children valuable learning opportunities that come from appropriate increased freedom. Many successful artists and performers have related how they were told they never would amount to anything unless they "got a real job."

As parents, even though we believe it is our job to make decisions, we must remember that the child sometimes knows best what he needs for his personal journey into adulthood. One thing that influences a child's ability to trust his parents is being given reasonable amounts of responsibility and freedom to explore new territory. How many children find themselves as adults in unsuitable careers they chose primarily to please their parents?

When mistakes are made, children must be able to trust that their parents will respond in reasonable and constructive ways. Parents learn to trust their children by observing how they handle additional responsibility. Believe it or not, most children are willing to say, "You were right, Mom," as long as they don't have to hear "I told you so." And children often are apprehensive about some of their choices. Children often will tread with some trepidation down unfamiliar roads, even though they'd like their parents to believe they know exactly where they're going.

Promises Made, Promises Broken

Building a trusting relationship involves learning to listen and respond to your children in ways that communicate honesty, respect and understanding. Children want to feel that you care about them and sincerely wish to help. Many people talk a good game, but make promises they don't keep. Failure to appreciate the impact of broken promises can have a devastating effect on a relationship. Although the person who fails to keep a promise may be quick to accept his own excuses, the disappointed one may be left feeling angry, hurt and unimportant. When someone repeatedly breaks promises, he risks losing credibility. The one who is continuously disappointed gradually will lose trust in that individual, and may experience difficulty developing trusting relationships with others.

People who believe promises are made to be broken shouldn't be making them in the first place. If someone feels compelled to make a promise, inherent in this sacred form of commitment is acknowledgment that something is very important to somebody else. It is an injustice for someone to recognize this and then casually make a promise for which they make little effort or do not intend to keep. It reflects both insensitivity and a lack of understanding about the relationship between promises and trust.

In divorced families, this issue is dramatically heightened. Even well-adjusted children struggle with their feelings about the family breakup. When promised visits are cancelled or money is late or never arrives, children understandably feel less important. Loving words in the absence of significant behavioral change won't re-establish trust or increase self-esteem.

There are many reasonable alternatives to making promises, since promises usually are construed as absolute commitments. Because we live in a world with fewer and fewer absolutes, parents often unwittingly set themselves up to break promises despite their best intentions. One rule of thumb is to try not to make promises under duress. These are more likely to be broken when the stress remits.

You just discovered under your bed an old and forgotten winning lottery ticket that you confirm is worth millions. You have only one hour to cash it in before it expires. Your sixteen-year-old son has hidden your car keys and refuses to return them unless you agree to buy him a motorcycle with your winnings. Being the devout capitalist that you are, you promise him the bike of his choice if he immediately returns your keys, which he does happily. Not only are you unlikely to keep your promise, but guess who now is going to have to work his way through college and walk to class.

Although this example is far-fetched (who really looks under their bed), many parents do make promises to their children just to maintain peace. It is a tenuous peace until it's broken after the promise suffers the same fate. If you decide to make a promise to your child, it is helpful to provide yourself with some latitude such as, "We will visit your hamster's grave, but I can't tell you exactly when. It will be within the next month." This approach often works well as long as it doesn't become just another delay tactic or a way to avoid paying your respects altogether. But if promises are too vague and noncommittal, parents should expect their children to doubt their sincerity and pressure them for a more definite answer.

The simplest solution to the problem of broken promises is to keep them, or at least to show a good faith effort when you cannot. Substitutes for broken promises such as, "I'll try my best," or "I'll let you know when I have the time," will be no more satisfying to the child than an Eggbeaters omelet is to an adult who lives for the real thing. Parents first must establish a good track record of keeping promises if they want their promises to be taken seriously by their children. A solid track record also allows for forgiveness and understanding if you occasionally blow a tire. Because promises always are related to the issue of trust, the implications are serious should they be broken. Even if you forget that you made the promise, all children possess total recall when something they value is threatened.

When an adult is hurt by a broken promise from another adult, at least he has the benefit of age and experience to help soften the blow. But children are vulnerable and may be devastated by a broken promise, which to an adult may seem inconsequential. For example, if a child only sees a noncustodial parent infrequently, a last-minute cancellation of a trip to Dairy Queen can be highly upsetting.

Because children tend to idealize their parents, on whom they depend for protection, guidance and nurturance, sometimes they make excuses for them when they fail to keep their promises. Children shouldn't have to bear the burden of making amends for a parent's broken promises.

* * * * * *

"One rule of thumb is to try not to make promises under duress."

* * * * * *

One risk is that a child might minimize his own needs to help him cope with his disappointment. This may be wrongly interpreted by his parents that he handles disappointment well. Some children reinforce this perception by suppressing their feelings and even owning the problem by believing that promises are broken due to some fault or inadequacy of their own. This can become a vicious cycle that can cause irreparable harm to the self-esteem of the child and the parent-child relationship.

It is inevitable that children will experience many disappointments in life, and it is important to teach them sometimes to forgive and forget. But in families where promises are made lightly and often broken, children might forgive, but seldom forget. When a child learns he cannot trust what his parents say, he may choose to stop listening to them altogether.

I Really Mean It This Time

Many parents are sincere when making promises to children, but become overwhelmed trying to balance the demands of daily life. Although some children have suffered more than others from parental instability, all children are sensitive and vulnerable. Despite their willingness to often give their parents the benefit of the doubt, their tolerance for "I forgot" or "I don't have enough time" is definitely limited. Even the word "can't" is a risky word, because usually children are correct in thinking, "He could if he wanted to." A child who has heard too many times, "I'll make it up to you," eventually figures out that his parent really is "making it up."

During the years I worked with hospitalized children in crisis, I was dismayed at how frequently the themes of broken promises and mistrust played major roles in their difficulties. Their tendency to minimize the damage being done by their parents often made it difficult for them to understand the roots of their out-of-control behavior. Often, the crisis of hospitalization precipitated the resurfacing of an absent or inconsistent parent who again was promising to maintain a consistent presence in the child's life. The elated children would unrealistically raise their hopes, despite my cautioning them and their parents not to

"Children shouldn't have to bear the burden of making amends for a parent's broken promises."

rely on promises they previously couldn't fulfill. Children would try to convince me that their parents' promise of "I mean it this time" was at last sincere. Too often, a child was devastated when her parent failed to follow through with a promise to finally be there for her.

Despite the devastating disappointment, many children held onto the slimmest thread of hope that someday their absentee (physically and/or emotionally) parents finally would make them a priority. The more they remained in denial, the more difficult they were to treat. In some cases, even a dramatic turnaround on the part of the parents was insufficient to undo the damage already done. I often was uncomfortably pessimistic about the chances for many of these children to develop and sustain meaningful and trusting relationships in the future.

The Lyin' King

My interest in exploring the phenomenon of trust was heightened after treating a 10-year-old boy I'll call Alex. Although he never knew this, he earned the nickname "the Lyin' King" for his propensity to tell fantastic lies in a convincing fashion. Alex was intellectually limited and suffered significant speech and language difficulties. I often had trouble comprehending what he was saying and I had to use simple sentences for him to be able to understand me. Alex was referred to me because he had difficulty controlling his temper.

Alex usually was pleasant and cooperative and he was motivated to handle responsibilities in an age-appropriate manner. I could depend on him to accurately report his progress on mutually agreed upon goals. He agreed that sometimes his behavior was inappropriate, but he often felt powerless to change it. It seemed ironic to me that this young man, who seemed so straightforward and genuinely honest, was capable of telling some of the most outlandish lies I had ever heard. These lies ranged from claiming he found a five-dollar bill on the street to his millionaire uncle promising to buy him a Corvette on his seventeenth birthday. As it turned out, these were some of the more believable ones.

I pride myself on being an astute clinician, but after working with Alex for a while, I began to question which one of us was intellectually limited. I initially was taken in by his stories (that sounds so much nicer than calling them lies), and soon it became clear that I had vastly underestimated the richness of his imagination and his deft acting ability. Arbitrarily and seemingly without provocation, he would make up stories he insisted were true. He had perfected his act to a point that he could sense when I was skeptical, so he would embellish the story in an attempt to make it more believable. Below is a typical dialogue between the Lyin' King and me:

> *Dr. B:* "So what did you do at school today?"
>
> *LK (Lyin' King):* "Nothing!"
>
> *Dr. B:* "Nothing? Why not?"
>
> *LK:* "Because we didn't have school today."
>
> *Dr. B:* "No school today? Why not?"
>
> *LK:* "The heat broke."
>
> *Dr. B:* "Was the school closed for the whole day?"
>
> *LK:* "Yup!"
>
> *Dr. B:* "So what did you do?"
>
> *LK:* "I played basketball with my friends."
>
> *Dr. B:* "Was it fun?"
>
> *LK:* "Yeah, my team won every game."

During the early phase of treatment, we had many similar conversations that sometimes made me skeptical of what he reported. Because his parents didn't identify lying as a significant problem, I initially didn't feel compelled to check with them every time I became suspicious of his stories. When his embellishments became more outrageous, I began including his mother in sessions to help me assess his veracity. Although Alex was aware that he was lying, he didn't protest when I suggested his mother participate in his sessions. I began reporting to her statements like, "Alex tells me he was not in school today." More often than I care to admit, she would look at me, grin slightly and say, "And you believed him?"

Before long, I realized the extent to which Alex was trying to take me for a ride in his lie mobile. It was powered exclusively by fiction and was a finely tuned machine capable of getting from two to ten lies per session. Because I tend to pick up on things quickly, especially after repeatedly being hit in the face with them, I was able to bite my tongue before blurting out to his parents, "Alex tells me he was just named the starting center for the New York Knicks. You and your husband must be very proud."

In fairness to me, I didn't fall for every lie Alex told. We made great progress in this and other areas. But the Lyin' King continued to rule for a while, even after I decided it was time to coax him to relinquish his throne. My main concern was to teach him that he could hold a prominent place in the jungle without feeling that he always had to lie. As I began to understand him better, I realized that there were some recurring themes in his lies that could serve as valuable clues to help me understand why he felt so compelled to lie.

Usually when he lied, he presented himself as excelling in a particular area or dominating someone else physically or mentally. Another repetitive theme was that he didn't have to attend school. Sometimes he would choose someone else as the protagonist of the lie, but the themes usually remained the same. In those cases, he became an eyewitness who swore that what he reported actually occurred. The day he told me that he and his uncle went fishing and his uncle caught a two-headed fish as big as my office, I knew it was time for me to reel Alex in.

The focus of treatment became how Alex often felt inadequate in school and in life. We agreed that many of his lies represented his wish to feel more competent and confident in his abilities. Because he knew that he often didn't measure up to his peers, he retreated into fantasy so he could feel more successful and powerful. Convincing people that his lies were true accomplished these goals. As our relationship grew and intensified, the issue of trust gradually took center stage. Alex told me he enjoyed our sessions and that he admired my professional status. Despite his fondness for me, he admitted that it was difficult for him to trust me to like and accept him with all of his limitations. It seemed that, by evaluating how I handled discovering when he lied to me, he was testing the strength of our relationship and deciding if he could trust me.

As his lies became more absurd, I was struck by how desperately inadequate he felt, and what a struggle it must have been for him to maintain an outward appearance of a self-confident and contented child. Although lying provided fairly effective protection from feeling overwhelmed, he realized that as he grew older, the more problematic this behavior would become. Over time, we were able to address some of his concerns and he began to feel relieved that, at least with me, he didn't have to pretend anymore. This opened the door for me to address his lying directly without his becoming overly defensive.

I first told him that I could understand why trust was such a major issue for him, but that I was still surprised at how easily he allowed himself to lie. We also discussed how most people are willing to accept honest mistakes, but not deception. Over several sessions, we discussed how this issue of trust had its roots in his feelings of inadequacy, and that his parents, teachers, peers and me all were affected. He began to realize that learning to accept himself as a total person would be key to developing trust in others and vice versa. I wondered aloud if he could control or cease his lying if he one day decided that this was important. He insisted he could if he "put his mind to it." We discussed how he had matured in many other ways since we began meeting, but that I still wasn't sure if he wished to be like his peers, who had learned long ago that lying is unacceptable. After considering this subtle challenge, he said, "If they can do it, I can do it."

We agreed to work out a simple plan. When I suspected that he was lying, I would ask him, "Is this a wish or the truth?" Because he usually kept his promises, he answered truthfully and, before long, he voluntarily began informing me when he lied. It finally seemed that we had developed enough mutual trust to make significant progress together. This technique also was used by his family with great success, and Alex was delighted to successfully break this habit, which had persisted for years.

❋ ❋ ❋ ❋ ❋ ❋
"Most people are willing to accept honest mistakes, but not deception. "
❋ ❋ ❋ ❋ ❋ ❋

Early on, when Alex began experimenting with telling the truth, occasionally he reverted to his old habit of lying, apparently to see if he would get caught. Usually he did and, to emphasize the consequences of lying, I subjected him to my version of the boy who cried wolf. When Alex would tell me something I knew to be true (such as cleaning up his room without being told), I would tell him I suspected that he was not telling me the truth. As you might imagine, he became angry and frustrated and insisted I verify his honesty with his mother. I responded that he was getting too old for me to always check with his mother, and that if he was going to make me guess when he was lying, I also would have to guess when he was telling the truth. Sometimes I probably would guess wrong, but it is a problem he created because he still reserved the right to lie.

He began to understand that I was now in control and that every time he lied, he was giving more control to me. This did not sit well with the Lyin' King, who was not used to having his power challenged, especially in his own kingdom. He gradually learned that telling the truth far outweighed the benefits of lying. Lying previously provided him with an exciting emotional outlet, but now it had become a burden he no longer wished to bear.

The key to my success with the Lyin' King was my determination to understand what compelled him to lie and to lay a foundation of trust. This made it safe for him to address important underlying conflicts, feelings and concerns that he had masked over the years. To get him to embrace change, I used humor to help him consider how absurd some of his methods were to gain admiration and respect. For example, when he told me about the two-headed fish his uncle caught, I responded by saying, "That's impossible, Alex, because I used to sell that kind of fish and they always have three, not two heads. You must have counted wrong. Knowing he trusted me allowed me to take such a risk without fear that he would feel belittled.

The Lyin' King saga demonstrates how developing trust can be a slow and arduous journey. After the Lyin' King developed trust in me, he was more than happy to abdicate his throne.

Mirror, Mirror, on the Floor

Some time ago, a mother told me she suspected her eight-year-old daughter Emily of breaking an expensive antique mirror, but Emily repeatedly denied it. This mother asked me what she could do to get Emily to tell the truth. She was struggling with how to punish her because she lacked indisputable evidence of her guilt.

I reminded her that her daughter actually might be telling the truth, because, despite visual enhancement, the videotape from the security camera remained fuzzy. Although her mother remained convinced of Emily's guilt, she conceded that a jury trial probably was not feasible because most of Emily's peers would be too busy playing to serve. I asked her to analyze whether she was more upset about her favorite mirror being broken or the possibility that her daughter might be lying. She identified lying as her primary concern. I told her she may never elicit the confession she desired, but that something good still could result from the incident. To help her focus on what questions to ask her daughter, I shared a favorite quote from the eighteenth century philosopher Voltaire, who said, "Judge a man by his questions rather than by his answers." Emily's mother initially was focused on extracting a confession from Emily. The next day, she conducted the following discussion with her daughter:

> **Mother:** "I have told you, Emily, that I believe you know how the mirror was broken. But because I have no proof and cannot be sure, I guess I will have to accept what you tell me. I do have a question I'd like to ask you, however. Okay?"
>
> **Emily:** "I didn't break the mirror, but what do you want to ask me?"
>
> **Mother:** "I would like to know that if you broke the mirror or are covering up for someone else who broke it, would it be hard for you to tell me what happened?"

Emily: "I think I would wait to see what kind of mood you are in."

Mother: "So sometimes telling the truth depends on how you think I'm feeling?"

Emily: "Sure, Mom. When you are in a bad mood, I try to stay out of your way."

Mother: "Why would you be afraid to admit something to me just because I might have had a hard day and am not in the best mood?"

Emily: "A couple of times when I told you something that upset you and you were in a bad mood, you yelled at me and brought up past things I did wrong that I thought we already had dealt with."

Mother: "Do I really do that?"

Emily: "Not always, but sometimes you do, and I can never tell when you will and when you won't. It's hard for me to trust you when you're like that."

Emily's mother was speechless. After mulling over what she heard for about an hour, she once again approached Emily.

Mother: "I can understand how you feel. I am really glad you could tell me how my moods affect your honesty. I'm sure it wasn't an easy thing to do. I never really thought about how my being in a bad mood could affect the trust between us. I guess I have some work to do. I would like to say one last thing about the mirror."

Emily: "Go ahead."

> **Mother:** *"It is possible that you too might think a little more about the mirror situation. If you know something, I promise I will control my reactions. And in the future, it's okay for you to say, 'Mom, you are not in the best mood, but I need to talk to you.' That will be my cue that, while I am listening to you, I also need to listen to how I'm reacting to you."*
>
> **Emily:** *"Okay, I'll think about it."*

Although, to my knowledge, Emily's mother never did extract the coveted confession, the dialogue that occurred raised their trust level and relationship to a higher level. Mother worked hard at keeping her emotions in check so that Emily would consider her more approachable. Emily began to test the waters and share minor transgressions with her mother, such as not finishing her homework. When she felt her mother was overreacting, she would say, "Mom, you are really getting angry about this." Instead of becoming defensive, Emily's mother learned to step back and even apologize at times. Both agreed that the levels of honesty and trust were enhanced as they felt more comfortable communicating with each other.

To update you on Emily's progress, I heard she is due to be paroled from prison sometime next spring after serving a lengthy sentence for contributing to the fracture of a mirror. She continues to maintain that she is innocent. Unfortunately, for Emily, she's had a great deal of time to reflect.

※ ※ ※ ※ ※ ※

Each of these illustrations share at least one common theme. Trust was a powerful issue that significantly impacted the quality of the relationships. It is much easier to offer prescriptions for discipline than for trust. The development of trust often is difficult to direct or assess. How relationships develop and life events unfold, are your primary barometers of trust.

For parents hoping to instill a high level of trust between their children and themselves, I offer this advice. Continually ask yourself, "What must it feel like to be my kid?" If most of the time a smile invades your face, you're probably on the right track. If you suddenly feel upset or concerned, then examine whether the process of trust has somehow been derailed. The good thing about trust is that, in most cases, it can be enhanced or rebuilt. But since your children grow up as fast as a speeding locomotive, there is precious little time to waste.

One thing is certain. Regardless of how much time, love and energy you devote to your children, it is impossible to undervalue trust. Everything a parent does potentially impacts this "T." If you forget this, your relationships with your children are sure to T**(rust).**

* * * * * *

Communication can be unpredictable and highly complex. Discussions that we anticipate to be antagonistic sometimes are unexpectedly calm. And interactions we expect to be without conflict can become battlegrounds. It is impossible — if you hope to live a spontaneous and enjoyable life — to remain continuously cognizant of all aspects of communication.

The five Ts are communication guidelines that will help you establish healthy parent-child boundaries. Practicing them will help you improve your ability to relate more effectively to people in all aspects of life. In addition, the five Ts are critical to helping you handle the granddaddy of all Ts – Teaching.

Face it. As long as you're raising your children — or simply breathing on this earth — school is never out of session. And the best teachers are those who relish their role as perpetual students.

Don't Drown in the Car Pool!

Epilogue

There is an old saying, "Man makes plans and God laughs." Even knowing that the events in our lives and the universe are ultimately out of our control, the human race is committed to discovering new ways to influence them.

The experience of raising children certainly is no exception. Parents can do their best to plan, protect and teach their children, but at some point all they can do is hope. Although hope springs eternal, it also can spring a leak.

What can parents do when this occurs? Although parents cannot control their children's destinies, they can learn to expect the unexpected and be prepared with tools to help repair the leaks. The creative tools offered in this book can help parents become more proficient at their craft. A harsh, unforgiving climate makes it difficult to build solid and enduring relationships. Remember that each parent possesses qualities that can be transformed artistically into a unique and rewarding style of parenting. Because of this truth, no individual book or collection of books on parenting can adequately meet every parent's needs. Parents must be willing to experiment and explore novel ways to relate to their children to identify what works for their family. Once discovered, it must be nurtured, refined and rehearsed so that it becomes familiar, comfortable, and everyone has a chance to adjust and benefit.

People continue to undergo changes on emotional, spiritual, physical and intellectual levels. Therefore, it is impossible for families not to change. It is possible, however, for people to minimize or ignore these changes and refuse to develop new attitudes and behaviors to effectively cope. Effective parenting, like life, is a journey, not a destination. And creativity is the compass that helps you to navigate your way through uncharted parenting waters. Remember, as much as you try to hold a steady course, at times all you can hope for is to hang on for the exhilarating ride.

The challenge of parenting cannot be understated. Day after day, as we parents jump through hoops to raise our kids to the best of our ability, life often feels like just another three-ring circus. So remember this. If you want to enjoy the show, you've got to be willing to clown around. While your kids are spilling soda and mashing caramel popcorn into your new carpet, remember to put life's pressures in perspective. After all, most stains can be removed without a trace. However, the parenting legacy you leave will last for generations.

END

Don't Drown in the Car Pool!

Creative ways to raise great kids

By Mark Berkowitz
with Verna Noel Jones

Name: _____

Address: _____

City: _____ State: _____ Zip: _____

Mail your check for $15 .45 (12.95 plus $2.50 shipping) to:
(Add $1.50 S&H for each additional book shipped to same address)

Indelible PRESS

P.O. Box 46154
Denver, CO 80201-6154

Fax your order to: 303-752-9289
Call: 303-649-6576
Order toll free at: 1-888-372-1613
Check out Dr. "B" at www.drbkids.com

CREDIT INFORMATION

Customer Signature: _____

Print Name: _____

Phone Number: (___) _____

Card Number: ☐☐☐☐ ☐☐☐☐ ☐☐☐☐ ☐☐☐☐

☐ VISA ☐ Master Card   Expiration Date: ___ ___

☐ YES! Please add me to your mailing list

☐ My email address is: _____

139

Don't Drown in the Car Pool!

Don't Drown in the Car Pool!

Share your creative tips with other challenged parents!

I am a creative parent because I..._____

_____

_____

_____

_____

_____

_____

_____

_____

_____

_____

_____

_____

_____

_____

_____

_____

_____

_____

_____

Send us your great ideas to Dr. "B" to share with other families.
Ideas submitted may be used in future materials and presentations.
Individuals submitting ideas will only be identified by first name,
city, and state of residence.

Indelible PRESS

P.O. Box 46154
Denver, CO 80201-6154

Or fax your idea to: 303-752-9289
Or Email your idea to: drb@drbkids.com
Check out Dr. "B" at www.drbkids.com

Don't Drown in the Car Pool!